T0001178

UNF#CK YOUR
BUSINESS

USING MATH AND BRAIN SCIENCE
TO RUN A SUCCESSFUL BUSINESS

JOE BIEL + DR. FAITH G HARPER

A People's Guide to Publishing,
How to Sell Stuff at an Event

Wallstreet Journal bestselling author of
Unf#ck Your Brain, Unf#ck Your Worth

UNF#CK YOUR
BUSINESS

USING MATH AND BRAIN SCIENCE
TO RUN A SUCCESSFUL BUSINESS

JOE BIEL + DR. FAITH G HARPER

A People's Guide to Publishing,
Howto Sell Stuff at an Event

Wallstreet Journal bestselling author of
Unf#ck Your Brain, Unf#ck Your Worth

UNFUCK YOUR BUSINESS

Using Math and Brain Science to Run a Successful Business

© Joe Biel and Faith Harper, 2023

ISBN 9781648411588
This is Microcosm #732
First Published November, 2023
This edition © Microcosm Publishing, 2023

For a catalog, write or visit:
Microcosm Publishing
2752 N Williams Ave.

Portland, OR 97227

www.Microcosm.Pub/Business

To join the ranks of high-class stores that feature Microcosm titles, talk to your local rep: In the U.S.
COMO (Atlantic), **ABRAHAM** (Midwest), **BOB BARNETT** (Texas/Louisiana/Oklahoma),
IMPRINT GROUP (Pacific), **TURNAROUND** (Europe), **UTP/MANDA** (Canada), **NEW
SOUTH** (Australia/New Zealand), **GPS** in Asia, Africa, India, South America, and other
countries, or **FAIRE** in the gift trade.

Did you know that you can buy our books directly from us at sliding scale rates? Support a small,
independent publisher and pay less than Amazon's price at **www.Microcosm.Pub**

A significant portion of the original text was published in 2021 as *A People's Guide to Business*.

LIBRARY OF CONGRESS CATALOGING-IN-PUBLICATION DATA

Names: Biel, Joe, author. | Harper, Faith G., author.
Title: Unfuck your business : using math and brain science to run a
    successful business / by Joe Biel & Faith G. Harper, PhD.
Description: Portland : Microcosm Publishing, [2023] | Summary: "How do you
    start and run a successful business despite the odds? This unique
    business guide teaches you practical-alongside emotional-intelligence
    and coping-skills that you need in order to overcome internal barriers
    to success no matter what type of business you are in. Joe Biel draws on
    26 years of business ownership and management experience to walk you
    through how to think like a business owner and keep your focus on what's
    most important. Dr. Faith Harper provides vital skills that aren't often
    lauded in business books, such as communicating your boundaries,
    overcoming imposter syndrome, and more"-- Provided by publisher.
Identifiers: LCCN 2022055330 | ISBN 9781648411588 (trade paperback)
Subjects: LCSH: New business enterprises. | Industrial management. |
    Decision making. | Strategic planning.
Classification: LCC HD62.5 .B4984 2023 | DDC 658.1/1--dc23/eng/20221117
LC record available at https://lccn.loc.gov/2022055330

MICROCOSM · PUBLISHING

MICROCOSM PUBLISHING is Portland's most diversified publishing house and distributor with a focus on the colorful, authentic, and empowering. Our books and zines have put your power in your hands since 1996, equipping readers to make positive changes in their lives and in the world around them. Microcosm emphasizes skill-building, showing hidden histories, and fostering creativity through challenging conventional publishing wisdom with books and bookettes about DIY skills, food, bicycling, gender, self-care, and social justice. What was once a distro and record label started by Joe Biel in a drafty bedroom was determined to be *Publisher's Weekly's* fastest growing publisher of 2022 and has become among the oldest independent publishing houses in Portland, OR and Cleveland, OH. We are a politically moderate, centrist publisher in a world that has inched to the right for the past 80 years.

Global labor conditions are bad, and our roots in industrial Cleveland in the 70s and 80s made us appreciate the need to treat workers right. Therefore, our books are MADE IN THE USA

CONTENTS

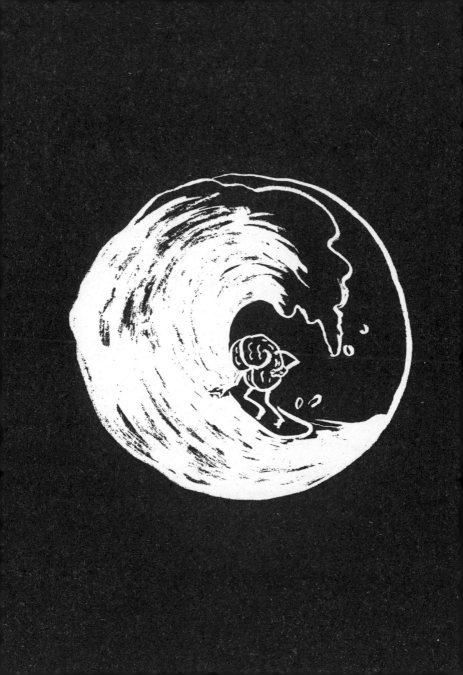

PROLOGUE

*I*n 2021, the *New York Times* advice columnist received a question from a young man who had obtained the "job of his dreams" but argued that he had hobbies and interests and no time to work 40 hours. Should he instead seek entrepreneurship, he pondered. I laughed out loud. The purest definition of *entrepreneur* is "someone who works 80 hours a week so they can avoid working 40." If he doesn't have time to work full time, he certainly doesn't have time to work double time as an entrepreneur, let alone as he simultaneously funds his startup and gets it off the ground.

Books like *The 4-Hour Work Week* and *The $100 Startup* have seduced our culture with this notion that entrepreneurs rake in the cash while sitting around eating bonbons on the beach. In reality, most entrepreneurs work more, borrow more, and fail more often than people with conventional jobs.[1] The Gallup Index reported in 2018 that 57% of business

---

1 *Entrepreneur* editor-in-chief Jason Feifer made an entertaining argument about why 90% of businesses fail. Feifer claimed that failed businesses worked for a few years before failing and that sometimes a business failed, but the entrepreneur succeeded at their *next* business, so the statistic was misleading. Groan. You can succeed if you follow my advice.

owners work *six days per week!*[2] *Harvard Business Review* reports that the average business owner works 72 hours each week!

Running a business isn't necessarily more difficult than having a job. "Burned Out Achiever" sent a "Dear Prudence" letter to *Slate*[3] that frames this issue magnificently:

> *My parents pushed me hard to achieve. It worked. I went to a letter school, qualified as a doctor, got a job in a busy hospital and have worked throughout the crisis. Today, I'm pushing 30, more than half a million dollars in debt, exhausted, and stuck in a misogynistic working environment where people treat me like dirt on a daily basis. By comparison, my brother ignored my parents completely, dropped out of school at 16, and is basically your classic stoner. He also started trading sneakers online when he was 12, graduated to Bitcoin, and is now a millionaire many times over in his mid-20s.*

Running a business is just a different skill set and it's not an instinctive one for most of us.. But, like

---

2 12% work seven days per week! Meaning the majority of business owners work *more* than someone employed by someone else!
3slate.com/human-interest/2021/10/resent-millionaire-stoner-brother-dear-prudence-advice.html

anything, the skills can be trained if you are willing. It takes time to break your own habits and see the bigger picture. So those are the skills we will work on in these pages.

This guide is for you if you are starting a business or have run one for years, whether you only have an idea or just feel stuck in your growth. Regardless if your vision is a taco truck or an herb mail order or a hardware store franchise or a hair salon, the same rules apply. However, if you simply want empty platitudes of encouragement or to cash in quick on your "big idea," this guide is probably not for you. We're just not that into blowing smoke up your ass to turn our own profit. We will focus on incremental growth and functional systems with the idea that you are building something to last. Even that egotistical dipshit Mark Cuban says, "If you have an exit strategy, it's not an obsession." If you aren't ready to quit your job, that's okay, you can limit your risk while getting a firm understanding of business part time. Most people I've encountered with a business are not "business people." They are people who have a magical passion but don't know, have, or follow the magic numbers or formulas necessary to succeed. They are merely passionate about the object and product of their business and either don't know or ignore the actual best practices and leave how it's run to chance.

When I was trying to consult with businesses, just about every single owner or manager voiced some variation of "But don't you think it should work this way?" which is a theoretical argument at best. What I think and what they think is irrelevant. We are dealing with reality in spades here. Instead of arguing how things should magically be, we'll take an up-close-and-personal look at every inch of how your organization is structured, what works, and what doesn't. It doesn't matter if you inherited the business from your great, great grandmother, started it five years ago, or have a hopeful dream to start something in the future, this guide will kick your ass and plant the seeds for making it work.

This book is co-written by Joe Biel—that's Joe speaking whenever you see a first-person pronoun— and Dr. Faith G. Harper. Joe's been running Microcosm Publishing for 27 years as of publication, and has learned every lesson in this book and then some the hard way. Faith is Microcosm's bestselling author (you may have heard of her book *Unfuck Your Brain*) and is mainly here with her therapist and brain scientist hats on, but she has a long and varied work experience, working for herself, for other companies, and for government agencies.

When I (Joe) was starting out, I sought a book to guide me. Everything that I found was boring, lacked comprehensiveness, and was more inspiration than information. Or as one reviewer put it about one of the books I read, "everything in this book is remarkably obvious." Most of them are selling the product of another business. Or a course that they created to help you make millions. It's not just a book, it's an invitation to part with more of your dollars. Maybe these authors don't have much in the way of answers. Indeed, most businesses are remarkably poorly run, and aren't great models for your own success. Here is the kind of advice that I needed 27 years ago, when I sought hard science that could form the foundation of my future success.

INTRODUCTION

*A*fter the first ten years of quietly running a successful business that I started with a few hundred dollars and no experience, people began coming to me for advice. They wanted to know how to solve problems within their own businesses. Because of my roots in punk rock, I heeded the mandate to create a trail of breadcrumbs so others could recreate my own success. Part of the social obligation of punk is to help others, each according to their needs and abilities. When it came to business, I had a greater knowledge base and better instincts than most, even when I didn't have much experience.

I started consulting with other businesses to help them work through their troubles. When I look at their practices, I ask "Why are you doing things this way?" and the answer is almost always "Well, we've *always* done things *this* way!" like I don't understand common sense. They can't see that it's not serving their goal while eating up valuable staff time, focus, and capacity.

They would continue their problematic behaviors and approaches and wonder why the issues didn't resolve themselves. In many cases, it felt like people would hire me just to have someone to talk to and complain with. While I was busy addressing the meat of their concerns, they were still shaking their heads, wringing their hands, and wishing things would be magically different.

After too many experiences like this, where I could solve problems in a matter of minutes yet nobody cared, I gave up on consulting and went back to running my own organization. But that pesky punk rock mandate to help others kept rearing its head, so I began creating a series of resources. This way, the people picking them up could read and apply my advice as they saw fit without me suffering the heartbreak of having to watch problematic practices persist.

Faith's experience is so similar it's almost like it's a universal problem or something. She's been asked so often about building a successful clinic, but by people who don't want to change anything they have already built. She gets that. It sucks to put in effort on something that isn't working so great. But it's cheaper than keeping all the janky workarounds you came up with, then leaning into what is required to be more effective.

THE RULES

*T*he hip hop artist Jay-Z, who has sold over 100 million albums and is worth over $800M, offers in his book, *Decoded,* business advice that he learned as a street drug dealer. Roughly paraphrased, he believes that there are three things that make a person good at business:

1. **The ability to do math in your head**

2. **Being a good judge of character**

3. **Making quick decisions**

I would add critical thinking skills, attention to detail, and a willingness to work hard, which Jay-Z also exhibits in force. Even if you have these skills naturally, you will need to practice and hone them as you find yourself in unfamiliar social situations with highly skilled negotiators. It doesn't hurt either to have a touch of grit and a lifetime of overcoming obstacles. You'll find yourself primed to solve problems as they come up.

There are nine very basic rules that inform all aspects of running a business. These are day-to-day rules that form your big picture guidance. This list began as a joke. In 2012, our warehouse manager would write down things that I would say with half seriousness on a public dry erase board. Within the next year they appeared in the employee manual. I figured that it'd be a good idea to refine them. After another year, my partner suggested that I should write a manual. Eight years later, I finally got around to it and the experience that I accumulated in the meantime made me both better at understanding the issues and imparting this wisdom:

#1 Believe in yourself. Just about everyone that I know has a confident exterior surrounding a deeply insecure core of their being.[4] These insecure people think that everyone else knows what they are doing except them, who snuck in by accident as an imposter who nobody has noticed yet, and every success so far was purely coincidental. If you're going to make it, take the time to evaluate your own successes, why they were successful, what bad habits you slip into, and make conscious and concerted efforts to replicate your successes. Fake it till you make it and all that. When you're talking to yourself—even out loud—there are no bad questions.

---

4 Faith wants to point out that, when left to fester, this can be the seed of a narcissistic personality disorder.

#2 Revisit your prime directive. When you start out, your path may be daunting, but it's very clear what goals and tasks are important. As you add activities, workflows, staff, and infrastructure, you will find that you are surrounded by tasks that do not move the needle towards the goal. You can go to work for a whole week, where you just spin your wheels, ending up nowhere closer to your supposed destination. For a lot of entrepreneurs who previously had regular jobs, you may not even notice this because so many jobs aren't about practical use of your time; they are about getting through the week. So it's vital to look at your leverage: how is *every* task that you perform or assign to someone else helping to get you closer to your goals? If it's not, is it vital?[5] If not, how soon can you get rid of it? Some things *seem* important or are fun, but with a bit of rigorous evaluation, you can figure out how to remove those obstacles from your path.

#3 Respect the math. Both Dr. Faith and Joe's best friend's little sister are statistical analysts. That means that they are paid handsomely to assemble

---

5 One example is filing taxes. Filing isn't vital to running the business but if you try skipping it for a few years, you will quickly find out that it's much easier to do it correctly and on time...even if it benefits none of your leverages.

complex data sets and analyze them. And yet, my friend's sister's number one complaint is that the actions of the people who hire her make no sense after seeing the information she provides. All decisions should be made based on data. The problem is that the people who hire her insist that she should find ways to lie with the data and demonstrate their conclusions, rather than them learning the actual facts. This is a problem for almost every business that Joe has worked with: they either don't know their own data, willfully ignore it, or massage it for their public-facing self while changing nothing. The number of times Faith has been asked to show statistics that show trends that didn't exist in the math is not a small number. This is so common in personal finance that psychologists study why people would hide their head in the sand. Spend the time to look at your own data and figure out what it means. Yes, the results are often uncomfortable or unpleasant but it's much better to work through your emotions before the results are catastrophic because you insist on continuing down the wrong path. Figure out what is producing the best results and how to repeat those results. Figure out ways to eliminate what is holding you down.

#4 No more accidents. This one has a multiplicity of meanings. We typically think of accidents like a shelf falling over or a person getting injured, but you want to expand that meaning in your mind to include choices that are unmindful. We know, mindfulness is one of those things that Buddists, therapists, and especially Buddhist therapists like Dr. Faith love talking about. But in this situation, we mean acting within intention in the present moment. Slow down your process, choose your words carefully, think about what you want to accomplish. If this seems like trite advice, think back on your own life, business or not. When did you Leeroy Jenkins yourself into some situation and make a big-ass mess that you could have avoided if you had just thought it through a tiny bit more? Faith's running joke is "good start... but keep thinking through a few more steps.". Think about the costs and compromises implicit in what you want to happen. Plan for them. Break every goal and task into actionable steps that you can work on a little bit each day. Nothing will feel inevitable this way. Think about where you want to go.

#5 Talk about your problems. Running an operation requires so many considerations and decisions that you will often get stuck. This is due to stress and capacity overload. While there's a certain trope of the complaining businessperson who has few problems to begin with, there's an incredible value to hearing yourself say something out loud and immediately realizing the solution. Sometimes this requires another person to listen and talk it over with, but usually you'll find that you are the one that comes up with the answer. In the tech industry, people will put figurines on their desks to talk out problem solving with.

When Faith was working on her doctorate, she was given excellent advice by one of her professors: tell people about your research. The same is true of business. Talk about it on the bus with a trapped audience. Not to be told in return how brilliant you are, but to be told, "Yeah, but how does that apply to queer couples?" or, "OK, but what if they have cats *and* dogs?" It's not that someone else knows your business better than you or knows more than you in general, but they have an outsider's perspective which can allow them to see the situation from a different perspective of someone living in it.

#6 Respect others but don't let haters get you down. Good business relies upon teamwork to function successfully. When you decide that you have to do everything yourself, you have failed. Working together means that you need to listen and accommodate others' wants and needs. At the same time, you'll find that your business isn't for everybody—nor should it be—and some people will have a painfully negative view of what you're doing. For example, a subscriber to our newsletter responded to say that we'd sell more copies of Faith's bestselling *Unfuck Your Brain* without the crass title. When we pointed out that we've sold over three million copies across all formats and the directness in the title is what makes it so popular, she responded "Yes, but do you think that's right?" Clearly, this book isn't for her.[6] And that's fine. But we also shouldn't change it for her because doing so removes what made it so successful in the first place. When we published the swear-free edition *Befriend Your Brain* in 2022, we knew that it would sell 90-95% fewer copies, but that it would reach and appease an audience we weren't already accessing. This decision was based on feedback from people who loved the book but worked in community organizations where

---

6 Also? The minute you think the world should change for your comfort level, you need to evaluate your own main character syndrome. Faith thinks pineapple on pizza is fucking disgusting. She isn't going to insist that you get pepperoni and black olive instead, but she is definitely not interested in your nasty-ass pizza. For the love of the Creator, if you don't like sweary books, don't read them.

it would never be approved for use because of all the fuckedy-fuckery verbiage inside. It wasn't a "do it my way" demand, but a thoughtful request that would help fill a community need. It's imperative to listen to your peer group but to moderate and consider their feedback, rather than allowing them to dictate your decision making. Take feedback as data. The real skill is figuring out which half of it to disregard, which half to implement, and how.

#7 Complain as necessary. One aspect of the above is that you will receive and filter out a lot of negativity being thrown at you for no other reason than people can be pretty damn shitty. Owning a business gets easier with time and experience but it's never not-stressful. Processing through that in *helpful* ways will be invaluable to your sanity and stress levels. The task is to be productive, not vent-y. Venting leads to more venting, folding in on itself like a mobius strip of misery. Venting doesn't move the needle. Processing with someone you trust and respect is huge. Talk to your truth tellers and listen to their answers.

Another incredibly important useful tool is journaling. With a pen and paper if you can do so (it completes a neural circuit in the brain that doesn't happen with typing on a device). Dump it out. *Then* make it useful. Faith suggests the spot-check inventory delineated by Julia Cameron in her book *The Listening Path: The Creative Art of Attention*. Julia recommends asking yourself (*and answering for yourself*) the five following questions:

1) What do I need to know?

2) What do I need to accept?

3) What do I need to try?

4) What do I need to grieve?

5) What do I need to celebrate?

And yes, really answer all five if you are looking to move the needle. Question four helps you release whatever you need to release in order to do the first 3 things. What *do* you need to grieve about a bad day in business? Maybe it's invested time with no return. Maybe it's a review that feels unfair. Then Question 5 centers you back into your positive intentions.

And then if you tend to have pretty sticky negative cognitions (many of us do . . . brains are wired for protection, and over-attending to possible negatives are good for staying alive), gratitude journaling on top of this process can also be enormously helpful. Some people write down three things they are grateful for every day as a habit, which is awesome. But keep in mind that doing the exact same exercise every day will eventually make it less effective, so explore and mix things up. Faith has a slightly different version of this that helps keep the process fresh, which you can print out yourself.[7]

#8 Drink iced tea (or other suitable beverage). While coffee is the old office standby, I drink sixteen ounces of iced tea every day at work. What you drink isn't important. I mean, tea is best but whatever. But you need a ritual. We are wired for them, and they're soothing. It creates some breaks in your day and helps ground you. while you're working that performs a function beyond keeping you hydrated or caffeinated. For some people this is accomplished by cleaning, walking, or stretching—all of which serve similar purposes—but the advantage of a beverage is that it's more adaptable and less of a distraction from what you're focusing on. Spending some time with your beverage is taking a break for a few seconds from the constant imperative of performing and responding to things. Use this time to become a bit more proactive than reactive. Most of my best

7 faithgharper.com/worksheets-and-printables/

ideas were concocted while drinking iced tea. So use this time for more than just loading up on caffeine. Focus on your muse while creating a little space between stimulus and response. Think of your time with your iced tea like a collaborative office sounding board meeting, where you problem solve, refine, and hone the challenges that you are facing. Instead of dissecting the minutiae and semantics of how the critic on your Facebook or Yelp page is wrong, drink your iced tea, and reframe the issue to how you see it.

#9 Don't drive faster than the car in front of you. Respect what is going on around you. Many businesses try to behave as though they exist in a bubble—because it feels that way in your head. Maybe you do this minute, but you won't the next. You exist within a localized and globalized set of economies, changing interests, and evolving set of cultural environments. Perhaps there's a current trend of excitement about clay pots or ferns, but it's unlikely to continue for many years. As a book publisher, sometimes I'll find that two competitors are functionally publishing the same book at the same time. Or in the case of public domain works, sometimes it's literally the same book and one publisher would be better served by canceling instead of losing money on the venture. Read the news and stay current about your industry as well as how your world is shifting. You won't catch everything but you will notice way more obstacles with your eyes open.

#10 Don't stop believin'. When you have a business, it becomes your job to become its champion and evangelist. If you don't care, no one else will. You embody the brand. You need to focus on *this* business because you believe in it more than the other business ideas that you decided against. This belief will be tested periodically during your career, sometimes multiple times per day. So you need to remind yourself to see the forest through the trees at all times. You can't do this with your face pressed against the bark. It's your job to redirect others to see the big picture and goals when they get confused, get cold feet, or start to doubt the modus operandi. One of Faith's favorite things to teach in career counseling is that the best predictor of career success is passion and interest in what you're doing. Not skills and not capacities. Wanting to do something means that you are more likely to do it well. So, breathe, reboot, find a better idea. And let's face it, if you don't believe in what you're doing, what are you doing here, reading this?

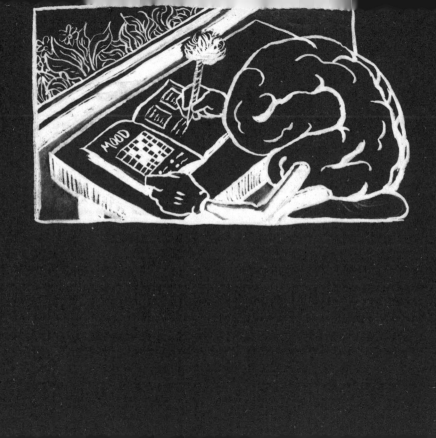

Part 1:

Make a

Plan

hether you are starting out or lost in the weeds of an existing business, the most important thing that you can do is to understand what is working, what isn't working, why things are or are not working, establish some goals, and then actualize that plan. Let's break this down into manageable pieces.

HOW DO I KNOW IF MY BUSINESS WILL WORK?

The "correct" way of proving that your business will work is called a "business plan." A business plan is a series of biased, made-up numbers that tell the story that you want to communicate. A business plan evaluates the size of your total market, diagnoses and explains away your competitors, and then manufactures some optimistic numbers to convince your bank or the Small Business Administration (SBA) that you are worthy of a loan, despite your lack of history or proof. A business plan typically includes projections of cash flow over the next five years—things that you couldn't possibly know at this stage and certainly do not line up to reality in 99% of cases. That said, if you are a relatively new business and you need to borrow money from a bank, you will likely have to go through the slog of making a business plan. But for most people that's just busywork and you'd be better off researching any other aspect of your business.

Of course, before you start running things you need to establish a baseline that you are fulfilling people's needs and that your means of reaching them is working. I wrote out a 21-point program for establishing a basic viability threshold that we used for years, but that sounds really boring, it's a lot to read, and during the course of writing this, I simplified it to a single mathematical formula. To test if what you are doing would work, consider this equation:

(Supply) / (Demand) x (Credibility) x (Access) = How Successful You Will Be

If you are less trained in experimental mathematics, you may be looking for simple numbers to plug in there and know the answer. But success is variable, right? Like, your idea of what's necessary for success is much less than what the shareholders of Coca Cola demand for success, right? And while you could plug in concrete integers here, this formula is much more useful for getting a general idea. You don't have data to plug in yet if something isn't tested, and you really only need a broad idea that something is viable.

Supply is how many other organizations are already offering your service or a similar one. If you are a hairdresser, you don't need to compete with salons thousands of miles away but you might have to compete with other local fashion and makeover services. If you are making artisanal dog treats, you could conceivably ship them all over the world, so you compete against every other dog treat manufacturer—corporate and artisanal—to varying degrees. You probably already know the intimacies of your exact market because you picked a business category that you are so passionate about. You picked a pursuit that you'd rather do than work a day job for someone else, right? Your passion is useful in your market analysis. Who are the notable players?

Demand is how popular what you are doing is. While there are upwards of one million self-help books in print, there are also many people who devour one after another endlessly. If they don't find the answers they want or language that makes sense to them in the first one, many people read another and another, slowly making sense of the world. Crystals went from something that a very niche set of people focused on to invading the mainstream through Instagram influencers. Every resident of the

U.S. has to file income taxes and many of them will hire a tax accountant to do so, so the market is huge and underserved. Similarly, most people purchase their food from a grocery store, based either on what is closest to their home or what reflects their values. On the other end of the spectrum, you have high-end products for a very small audience, like fine art. Very few people purchase original oil paintings to hang on the wall in their homes, but because these are original, one-of-a-kind works, they command very high price tags.

Credibility is the trustworthiness and reliability that you need to make a sale. When you buy a car or choose a college, most people make that decision based on the credibility of the brand. If you are making nutritional supplements, did a doctor or celebrity in your field approve those claims and their uses? Do you have household name recognition or certification of some kind? Or conversely, did your company or spokesperson suffer a scandal that led your fans to question your values? When Chip Wilson, founder of Lululemon, made public comments that some women don't look good in his clothes because their bodies were the problem, public outcry destroyed the company's credibility because of this and other sexist and fatphobic comments. Wilson resigned in order to insulate the company from things that he had said and so that the brand could move on without the baggage of lost credibility. I found it funny that the CEO of Ambercrombie made comments that "ugly people" don't look good in their clothes, because that's interpretable. If I look good in those clothes, am I pretty? In some cases, like motivational speaker Tony Robbins, the only credibility is the longevity of his work, with various people having vastly different experiences of how helpful his practices are. Consider how credibility plays a role in your own business and how it impacts your chances of success. In most cases, the credibility of a small, local business is tied most directly to word of mouth, Yelp and Google reviews of your business, and direct referrals from previous customers. Think about what you consider when you hire a plumber or a lawyer. You don't need the best. You need someone who can perform the work that you need. But when you go to a restaurant, are three stars enough or do you need four? Typically, a recommendation from a friend carries more weight than reviews from strangers!

Access is your ability to reach the people that would benefit from what you do. How will you reach people who will support you? Most people decide between the gas station closest to their house and the cheapest one across town. If you are opening a gas station, how many people live nearby? Since grocery stores are vast gatekeepers to so many consumers, they have rigorous processes for determining which products are appropriate for their shelves. If you're relying on grocery stores to sell your product, you may need broad advertising to the general public, like a TV ad or social media influencer. Do you have an adequate budget for that or will you have to wait for organic buzz to spread on its own? If you are launching a magazine for CEOs, do you have names and addresses? If you are offering cleaning products for medical equipment, you'd likely need to find customers at trade shows where you can locate numerous medical supply companies at once. If you make clothing for parakeet owners or accessories for muscle cars, do you have relationships with large groups of those consumers or with media and retailers that reach the appropriate audience? If you supplement public transportation for the city government, do you have relationships within the transportation office?

So for example, Dr. Faith Harper's private practice benefits from an insufficient supply. Meaning, there simply are not enough therapists practicing right now while the demand for these services is increasing. Similarly, the fact that millions of people have bought her books vastly increases her credibility. She's virtually a household name in therapy circles and gets requests for private counseling constantly. The only downside is access. Dr. Faith can't practice in states where she is not licensed, which, when you are an internationally popular author, is most places. Her business would be a great one to invest in.

On the other hand, if I was going to open a bike shop in Portland, the equation is a bit different. The supply of shops is rather vast, often with more than one per neighborhood. Demand for these shops is relatively stable but most consumers are loyal to a shop already, and would only go somewhere new out of necessity. Credibility is reliant upon word of mouth and can take years to properly establish. Access to explain how you stand out and why customers should choose you is a real struggle. So even if you are legitimately the best bike shop in Portland, your chances of success are not stupendous and you are going to have to fight very hard to show people that this is true.

If you cannot sell something, it always comes down to a failure in one or more of these things: too much competing supply, not enough demand, not enough credibility, or insufficient access.

People buy things from you because it solves a problem that they have. That problem may be physical, mental, emotional, spiritual, or societal. What problem are you solving? Why are you qualified to solve it? What are the material payoffs of your solution? When I taught a class at Portland State University, a student argued with me that he publishes fantasy novels, which have no value proposition. Another student interrupted him before he finished his sentence, "You're selling entertainment and a temporary escape from a difficult day." He's right. Even if your value proposition is somewhat inscrutable or hard to pin down, it's there.

People miss opportunities because they look right through them, especially if they went to college and are classically trained about how to interpret everything through the status quo. Reporter David Epstein says that the best advice he received when he worked as a fact checker was to read everything backwards and interpret every fact in reverse order, where he would invariably find leaps in logic.

Inevitably, anyone that creates something does so by looking at the same problems in a new way.

When Zappos was launched, the popular belief was that nobody would buy shoes online because consumers "need" to try them on, necessitating brick and mortar retail. The founders challenged this notion by walking over to their neighborhood shoe store, where they took pictures of the shoes on the shelves, created a website, listed the shoes, created very customer-friendly return and service policies, and waited to see if people would order. When the orders began flooding in, they walked back over to the shoe store, bought the shoes, shipped them off, and continued the experiment. They didn't make money on those early shoe sales, but that wasn't the point. They were establishing "proof of concept," which is to say, they were making sure that their idea worked before they built out their infrastructure to a tremendous scale.

You should do the same thing. Before you begin building infrastructure or investing anyone's money, make sure that your idea solves a problem that people have in a way that is agreeable to them. Despite better durability, resolution, sound, and image, BETAMax tapes failed to catch on because they weren't solving a problem. VHS was more prevalent, already distributed to most homes, and cost was a greater factor than quality. As you can see, people are less interested in invention or innovation and more interested in how said ideas solve their problems. After organizing my to-do list on paper for decades, I was slow to accept that a smartphone could synchronize my calendar and planner with all of my computers but now I don't know what I'd do without that solution.

You *always* want to start small in order to get your footing, figure out your metrics, and aim to grow 25% incrementally larger every month for the first two years. I've seen *way* too many self-funded upstarts produce far too much inventory and go bankrupt because they cannot afford customer outreach. It's easy to get stars in your eyes. But, it's much better to sell out and tell customers "Sorry, too much interest. We'll make more." Few things are as demoralizing as failing to attain your own unreasonable expectations.

Test your idea in a localized fashion. If you grow squash, set up a stand for one weekend before committing to a year stuck behind a booth at farmer's markets or opening a store. At Microcosm, if we are unsure of a new book or it goes too far in a new or untested direction too fast, we publish a zine first. It's less work, much less risk (it costs us 99% less) and the feedback (or deafening silence) informs if we make it into a book at all, and more importantly: *how* the book is developed.

Listen to feedback, learn from the experience, and ask people what they think before going big. This is one of the best lessons that you can take from the world of tech. Often, the ideas that work will be discovered through joking or sheer accident, rather than isolating cold, hard logic. The pacemaker was invented when John Hopps was trying to create a solution for hypothermia but instead discovered that the heart could be caused to pump blood through stimulation in 1951. Today, that accident keeps 4.5 million people alive. Rather than sticking to your vision, be willing to listen, adapt, and refine your ideas until they are solving a problem—even if you cannot see how right away. No idea is as painful as the great one that is too stagnant to catch traction.

WHAT PROBLEMS ARE YOU SOLVING?

Most people who have had a job will tell you that they have most of the solutions to their employers' problems, but are categorically forbidden to implement them. It's above their pay grade. They aren't allowed. Sometimes this is because these new ideas may not fit into the larger strategic goals and movements of the bigger picture, and the employee doesn't have the information or perspective needed to steer the company. But many other times, this is a matter of company culture being resistant to changes. Each time they ask their boss about these changes, they are sternly told "no." A friend's husband is in charge of a large manufacturing operation. The sales team sells much faster than manufacturing can produce things, every job is custom, there is no software to manage the manufacturing specs, and new customers are frequently prioritized ahead of orders that have been waiting. So the backlog gets bigger and bigger every month. My friend's husband has approached his boss many times to express what he would need to make this functional: more staff, proper software to organize, less demanding salespeople, greater availability of materials, uniform builds, etc. But the head of sales is close friends with the top brass, so the backlog worsens and my friend's husband is looking for a new job. The company can't see the impossibility of this task because they are so focused on sales and growth. Instead, they just apply more and more pressure on an impossible chore. You probably have plenty of examples of easy-to-spot problems in managerial thinking from your own jobs. It's easy to see what is breaking down when you are the one who has to actually do the job. Management has a tendency to be siloed, seeing the operation only through income, expenses, and growth.

Harvard Business professor Clayton Christensen makes the case that this sort of rigid institutional thinking has caused the utter downfall of entire industries. We can blame millenials for the downfall of fast/casual restaurants, or we could pay attention to why they don't go there. He says that it's not that entire companies or industries are too oblivious to see themselves driving off a cliff in their final years, it's that institutional mindset forbade leaders from pivoting.

Christensen's favorite example is that of computer disc drives. In the 1970s, computer mainframes used a 14" disc and rebuked the offer from a new manufacturer to switch to 8" drives, which stored less information. Instead the 8" drives were used on minicomputers that were much more affordable. Then, both mainframes and minicomputers ignored the rise of personal computers, which used 5 ¼" discs in new drives, and eliminated the need for their more expensive predecessors. By the time mainframe and minicomputers pivoted, personal computers already controlled the bulk of market share and it was too late. Personal computers solved problems better for consumers and so 5 ¼" disk drives drove the others out of business—even though they stored more data. Forty years later, you'd be hard pressed to find a competitor that can hold a candle to a solid state secondary storage device that fits in your pocket.

In some cases, there are often good reasons not to change. Microcosm once employed a book designer who was intent on turning us into a font creation firm. Yes, we could do that, but adding this aspect to our operation does not work in tandem with any other aspect of our business. It only takes us away from what we are good at and leads us into the unknown.

Be great at one thing, rather than doing a lot of different things of various quality. Faith has two post-doctoral certifications that seem very disparate. One is in sexology and one is in clinical nutrition and each involved hundreds and hundreds of hours of additional study. Are they actually disparate? No. She's a trauma therapist and they improve her skills in helping people by creating new pathways of support. Like her, ask yourself if a new idea or pursuit fits into your existing core competencies. Does it require additional staffing and research, or is it fundamentally distracting from what you are excelling at? As much as it sounds like a good gimmick, you don't want to be a laundromat that is also a tanning salon. You want to pick the one that makes your heart soar, become great at it, and pursue compatible services. A salon could do nails and hair because those are extensions of beauty and appeal to the same customers. A laundromat could double as a dry cleaner.

But when the two components don't build upon each other, you are destabilizing yourself. Microcosm used to offer custom printing, but as we grew, we had one set of customers who bought books and another who needed printing. When we'd get printing orders, I'd have to take a break from my routines, go down to the basement and print, wash out the press, clean up, and go back upstairs to catch up on my vital work. One business only distracted from the other. It was slowing me down instead of building upon itself.

Mass production model
ex. Trade book publisher with small profit margins
Advantage: Scalable

Automation model
ex. Setting up and owning a business with outside management
Writing books published by other people
Advantage: Passive income

Service-oriented/Labor-intensive model
ex. Custom publishing, Consulting, author services, technical publishing
Advantage: Bigger profit margins

At a mental health conference in DC, a woman picked up a slender book and asked "How much does it cost to publish something like this?" Her question was malformed, borne of so many implicit, wrongful assumptions. My business partner furiously shook her head at me, indicating not to answer objectively, but it was too late. "That one cost us about $15,000," I said. The woman looked horrified, like she had seen a dishonest ghost. "You really are charging too much," she spouted back. "It can't cost that much to make this little book." The reason that she didn't receive the answer she wanted and judged us so harshly is because she was asking the wrong question. She assumed that our service was taking money to publish books, as many "author services" companies do. Whereas, we make money by selling books and paying the author. Many, many people have suggested over the years that we create an additional service, taking money from authors to publish books. In reality, the woman was right, the costs of these services do not justify the lack of rewards. Our field is very competitive, the industry advantage is in scale, and we are better focused simply on selling books. The correct response would be "There are lots of companies that offer services like that, but we don't and I'm not familiar with who to recommend." But I can't explain that to a stranger who is intent on this and has a certain worldview. And again, it's much better to focus on the service that you are good at than to get lost in all of the things that you could be doing.

Another pitfall is approaching a problem backwards. I once met two men taking business classes, intent on opening a Christian bookstore in the mall. In their minds, the one across the street from the mall wasn't sufficiently evangelizing, so instead of determining whether or not there was sufficient demand for adding another competitor within one mile, they started with their conclusion that another store was needed and moved backward from that. Fortunately, for their bank accounts, the store never opened. If I was intent on opening a direct competitor, I'd first research population concentrations of people who would support such a store, establish methods of outreach (in their case, churches and other Christian organizations), and then find a location centered between them. In an even more disastrous example, in 1998, a major pharmacy chain researched "Best location in Ohio" and opened a branch across the street from a competitor where thousands of cars go by daily. The problem was, they had to demolish a downtown city block to do so, costing hundreds of thousands of dollars for the land alone. Trouble is, cars don't buy pharmaceuticals and the location was difficult to access. The new store was a ghost town and went out of business within five years. It's okay to have goals but you don't want your goals to take you away from best practices.

Understand the feelings of your fans without reacting too quickly. When ebooks were gaining steam in 2011, the entire book publishing industry panicked. While they had not prepared for this inevitability in technological evolution, they were now expecting the end of their industry as they knew it. Numerous embarrassing gaffs occurred, ranging from journalists declaring "the death of print" to people lamenting how they liked paper better, hoping that it would make "a comeback." People thought this shift was "obvious" and "inevitable," but ebooks never caught on, with their market share flat or shrinking over the course of the next ten years. Besides traveling business people and women over 60, consumers still largely prefer paper. Despite billions of dollars in infrastructure investment from Amazon and the industry's failure to plan, book publishing is largely unchanged. Paper book sales *grew* during those same ten years while ebooks shrank. Why? The vast majority of consumers do not find that reading digitally solves a problem.

The major advantage of being a small business is that you can see the future, implement changes quickly, and turn on a dime. A friend went to school to become a photographer. After years of studying the art and science and shadowing numerous real estate, portrait, and wedding photographers, he thought that his career was actualizing. To pay the bills in the meantime, he started an Ebay resale business out of his basement. Ten years later, the Ebay business was so successful that he also added a dropshipping business. Photography is now just a hobby because he can see where the demand is. He moved his business into a warehouse and hired employees. This comes down to the same supply-demand-access-credibility matrix. He can offer things that people want on a platform that they trust. On the other hand, despite my friend being a great photographer, there are many other photographers willing to work for free, trying to get their foot in the door in a very competitive marketplace. Photography fails to meet the requirements of the formula.

Recently, a friend contacted me. She has done everything from teaching at universities to childcare for the rich and famous to working in a tiny bookstore. Now, she wants to start a herbal business and had quite a few questions about what would be viable starting out in that industry. The answer is more obvious than it seems. When you have a new business idea, market research only goes so far. So does evaluating the supply/demand/access/credibility formula on paper, in isolation. You need to know enough about your subject matter and what works for people who are passionate about it. The best way is to be passionate about it yourself, so that you are proximate enough to instinctively know the answers to questions like "Would people buy healing herbs from a website?" Similarly, you understand what motivates people to buy. When you have your own passionate interest in herbal healing, you understand the needs of practitioners, you can identify holes in the market that others aren't serving, availability of what is desirable, and how to get it. You have subconsciously navigated all of these arenas yourself. So I responded to her question with my own question, "What makes you support the places that you buy herbs from?"

Despite founding a book publishing company, I once had no idea how to sell books, get placement in stores, or run an organization. But I had a tremendous amount of passion and determination. So I started setting up displays to sell books at punk shows. Quickly, I had dozens of repeat customers who formed a hardened fanbase for what I was doing. They started to ask smart questions, like "Where else can I find this stuff?" or even better "Do you know Suzanne, who buys books for Mac's Backs on Coventry? I bet she'd be really into this stuff!" And slowly, an infantile empire was born that became more and more adult. I listened to helpful feedback. I improved at my pursuit of the craft, rather than trying to tailor what I do in order to interest a different or "mainstream" audience. I knew that this was an underserved niche, because this is the niche that I, myself, was a part of. The best advice that I can give you is to find something that you are passionate about and carve an underserved niche within it, rather than trying to sell what you think "most people" want.

The most focused way to look at problem solving is targeted social media ads. You make a product, create a marketing video showing your product solving a problem, show the ad to people in specific demographics, and fill orders directly. Assuming that your product solves a problem and there is adequate demand, it's a great way to establish proof of concept for something new. What problem are you solving?

Good ideas are the ones that seem obvious in hindsight, where they fundamentally touched the appropriate people so deeply that everyone just felt like they were always there. Starbucks doesn't think of itself as a place to buy coffee. Its core focus is on creating a forum for authentic human interactions in a world where customers are lonely. In many places, Starbucks is one of the only venues to meet a stranger. A good business idea solves a problem with a solution that feels so obvious you wonder why no one else thought of it and implemented it already.

WHAT'S HOLDING YOU BACK?

*W*hatever unresolved personal baggage you are carrying around is exactly what will hold you back in business, leading you into bad decisions and blowing up essential relationships. Maybe you lose your head over mistakes. Maybe you can't bear to look closely at your finances. Maybe you struggle to tell people no. Maybe you panic and make hasty decisions, or freeze and struggle to make a decision at all. We're not going to get deeply into these issues in this book—you can check out Faith's many other books if you're curious, starting with *Unfuck Your Brain*—but we do know from experience that any amount of work you can do on your personal issues is likely to pay off immensely to remove these obstacles to your business' success.

In this chapter, we're going to focus on one of the most common ways people undermine themselves: imposter syndrome.

In the infancy of Microcosm, my greatest impediment was being a success apologist. I felt bad every time that we had a success. Even when people would congratulate me, I declined to take credit and suggested that it was a fluke—that I was further indebted to others who hadn't succeeded. It took me nearly ten years of this thinking to realize that it was absurd. When we succeed, we grow our communities and put money back into them. We support the people that we intended to support at all parts of the value chain. And success is the only way to give back—through teaching others and having more cash flow than we need for once.

My hangups about success weren't caused by a material resource inadequacy. They were caused by my upbringing and how I was raised to resent successful people. I had to overcome that in order to see the difference between perception and impact.

Similarly, you have things that are holding you back. These things are often difficult to recognize until you are moving. Even then, the brain has a way of explaining away your own bad behavior and decision making. I'm passing the torch to Faith to talk a little about why that is.

Faith here, bringing some clinical knowledge. Those of us who struggle with imposter syndrome struggle with a highly critical inner voice. Our own internal dialogue tells us we lack worth. We are more likely to think of all our successes as undeserved and tend to see ourselves as minutes away from being exposed as the fraud we are. This voice leads to emotional distress, depression, anxiety, addictions, distrust, self-criticism, and self-sabotage. These messages are incredibly common. Many people's inner critics have unhelpful comments about their work, like "You'll never be successful, so why even try? No one appreciates how hard you work. You are under too much pressure; you can't handle this stress. All your successes are just luck, you didn't earn them fairly."

Imposter syndrome was first operationalized by researcher Dr. Pauline Rose Clance, based on her work in clinical settings. She defines it as "a psychological phenomenon in which people are unable to internalize their accomplishments." She was initially studying women in high powered positions during the 1970s and 80s when this was still fairly rare. While anyone who fails to value their own contributions can view themselves as an imposter, research shows that it is especially prevalent in people who grew up in very dysregulated homes and experienced parental mistreatment. Disorganized attachment styles are incredibly prevalent among individuals with imposter syndrome.

If we have internalized a felt sense of being lucky rather than competent and hard working, we start exhibiting a constellation of specific characteristics. Maybe not all of them, in every case, but these are the commonalities described in Clance's work.

1. **The imposter cycle:** Mistrusting your abilities leads to either overpreparation or procrastination. Success then becomes a matter of effort or luck instead of skill acquisition over time.

2. **The need to be the best:** Many people with imposter syndrome found themselves often being the best in certain activities (school, sports, hobbies) growing up. As they move into larger spaces (college, workforce) they bump into other people that are better at certain things, which leads them to disregard how good they are because there is someone better . . . therefore they must be nothing.

3. **Superhuman aspects:** This need to be Superman/Superwoman/Superperson relates to the need to be the best in that is

about the enormous pressure we exert on ourselves. The difference here is that the need to be superhuman is more about perfectionism than being the best. You may have been the best in some instance but still feel that you didn't do as well as you should have, or that you fucked up in some way by not being perfect.

4. **Fear of failure:** If one needs to be the best, or even perfect, this leads to abject fear around all performance-based tasks. This leads to the cycle of overwork and overpreparation and complete exhaustion.

5. **Denial of competence and discounting praise:** What happens next? We know how hard we (over)worked and attribute all of our success to this fact, which keeps us from accepting positive feedback and praise. This isn't a false humility, but a true discomfort with our own success because we truly don't feel we deserve praise or any of our achievements, to the point we will argue with those who feel otherwise.

6. **Fear and guilt about success:** Because people with imposter syndrome truly feel undeserving, success feels either unearned or leads to anxiety that more will be expected of you, when you are already over preparing and are entirely exhausted over everything you produce.

We can't talk about imposter syndrome without talking about self-sabotage, can we? While many people with imposter syndrome continue to perform at extreme levels, others of us set ourselves up for failure again and again in preconscious ways. Psychologist Brad Brenner defines self-sabotage as any behaviors where we create harm and destruction around our own well-being and success. Karen Berg, who wrote *Your Self-Sabotage Survival Guide*, agrees, adding that it is the *direct result* of other negative mindsets (like, you know, imposter syndrome). Where imposter syndrome is often correlated with chaotic early childhood experiences and the attachment issues that have emerged from that, self-sabotage is often related to childhood trauma. It can show up as:

- Disorganization

- Indecisiveness

- Perfectionism

- Procrastination

Obviously, self-sabotage, burnout, and constant anxiety are going to affect your ability to run your business. More than how you perceive every situation, they are especially important to address because they will affect anyone you hire and work with, and potentially customers and vendors. Any maladaptive way that you view yourself is going to be evident and striking—especially if the onlooker views your business differently. It can be cute in your infancy to be surprised by your own success but over time, others won't have much patience for this. When I made a mistake after fifteen years of publishing, a customer said that it was okay and maybe I could reach out to other publishers and ask for advice since I'm "new." The fact that he was able to see me that way after so long was jarring and eventually eye opening. I turned the corner to realize that I needed to present myself like I know what I'm doing. Because I do.

If you're sending messages that success is unwanted or unrealistic, there's a real danger that people doing business with you and your own team may not take your business seriously or not even try to do their best. If you're sabotaging your own efforts or your employees' work, they won't stick around for you to sort things out. So address this early and thoroughly.

Losing your imposter syndrome does not mean you'll become a raging egotist or braggart. In fact, it's likely to result in becoming more realistic and even humble. Most importantly, you'll have a clearer understanding of what needs to be done and how your actions and beliefs affect your desired outcomes.

Managing these behaviors, like many mental health efforts, begins with self-awareness. Once we make our preconscious instincts conscious, we can build tools around better managing them.

First things first: Turn yourself into an autoethnographer of your own self-sabotage and imposter syndrome. It is going to feel a little silly to formalize the process, but trust us. You're going to have to formally walk yourself through this process for a bit before it becomes something you do automatically.

Step One: Test your hypothesis that you suck. However much you think you suck? Let's actually find out. Any time you are successful, write that shit down. But you also have to record the relative roles that luck, timing, and your own hard work played in that success. You think you keep falling into shit and finding the pony? Let's see if that's actually true or if you have more self-agency than you are giving yourself credit for.

Step Two: Pick your cheerleaders. Which people in your life give balanced, accurate, and loving feedback? Check in with them. *Not* with the people who haterade everything you do, or speak only from their own fears. And *also not* the people who tell you the sun shines out of your ass no matter what you say. Real success cheerleaders are the people who have your six in real ways. Ask them. Listen to their answers. Believe when they tell you you're killing it, not just when you suck.

Step Three: Model the success of people you admire. And here is the interesting part. Really admire them. Not just, "Hey, look at the dollar bills this gazillionaire made happen" but, "Look at how this person has held an ethical center and still does great and admirable work while also knocking out some amazing achievements." In Neuro-Linguistic Programming, this is called "success modeling." Look at the people who do shit really well and figure out their strategies. If you can, ask them what's worked for them.

And here is the most important part of success modeling. It's not just about watching what they execute perfectly. It's also watching how they handle failure. How they handle imperfection. How they handle not achieving what they want to achieve and how they learn and grow from those moments.

WHAT IS YOUR NICHE?

Who cares the most about what you're doing? What do you fundamentally have to offer them that nobody else does? Why do they care? How are you able to solve their problems better than anyone else? In what ways do you make their lives better? Make a list and hammer it down to its simplest form. Know this stuff on command, without reciting memorized bits, but because you understand the reasons for your success before you've even started.

Once you've got your niche figured out, write a one-sentence mission statement. You've inevitably got many keywords and brainstorms associated with your business. It's easy to get carried away with that and lose focus, burying the lede. Save those other ideas for later. Put them in a notebook, and put that on a shelf. You want to really just focus on *one narrative at a time*. It's much better not to attempt to say *everything* in your mission statement. When you spell out every last detail, you almost always bury all of the *important* ones.

Imagine you have to give an accounting for your work—your best work—and you only have five minutes to do so. Sounds crazy, except this is what a comic faces when she lands a guest spot on the *Tonight Show* for the first time. Or—smaller stakes—five minutes in a comedy club. Can you connect to an audience or not? Can you communicate this idea you have? Do you even have an idea to begin with? You've got five seconds to spell out why someone would care. In the business world this is called your "elevator pitch" and you can find all manner of advice about writing it.[8]

Ours is "Microcosm Publishing provides tools to change your life and the world." That hasn't changed in 27 years because it does what it needs to. Yours could be "Medicinal herbs for every ailment." If you were a tire shop it could be something like "We get you everywhere that you need to go!" In the beginning, your mission statement will be too long, so pare it down to its base parts. You can append the unnecessary sentences when people have a lot of interest in your operation and start asking questions, but for now, you need to know who you are and what you do!

---

8 zety.com/blog/elevator-pitch

Next, write a one-sentence vision statement. This part is mostly private. It's what you want to accomplish in time and it should be a goal so large that you may *never* accomplish it completely. For example, if you were an adoption agency, it could be "A home for every child within one week." If you manufactured bowls out of stained glass, you'd want to be "Featured in the finest restaurants and homes all over the world." And from there, you break those goals down into achievable, bite-sized goals. All of your goals should have deadlines—even if you don't always achieve them. Some goals should be modest, some goals should be very ambitious. The reason for this is two-fold: you want to feel like you are incrementally successful but if you set your sights too low, you'll never know what you can achieve. We have set some incredibly ambitious goals, like doubling our sales, and then far exceeded that goal ahead of schedule.

Consider your brand. How do you want it to feel? What are some associated keywords? A powerful brand, like Honda or Volkswagen, can sell cars for higher prices than Ford or Chevy, because there is a reputation implicit in the brand that the cars are better built and last longer. There is even pretension in these brands. Think of some other brands that are snooty or broadly democratic. What brands really masquerade their virtues on price or value? How have your competitors managed their brands? What makes your brand different? What do you want your brand to say about your work? Why? How much sass does your brand have? Are you spirited or bland? The most important aspect of managing your brand is being consistent. If you have an intern posting provocative photos on your social media one day and a serious statement about the doomed world the next, your followers won't know what to think. They will likely give you the benefit of the doubt and think you got hacked! Talk about your successes confidently. Frame everything in a message of positivity. Create a page on your website that tells your story. Create a logo that adds depth and dimension to your name. Consider your decisions this way or if this isn't your strength, hire someone to handle it for you.

When I founded Microcosm, I was a mess. I was a teenage runaway with zero clean clothes. Nobody wanted to loan me money or trusted me enough to believe that I would see this idea through. Today, we've sold millions of books and haven't changed our mission or vision one iota. It's just a bit more clearly defined. And more importantly, we have miles of successful track records for anyone who cares to research. We consistently perform better than most of our competitors because we consistently focus on all of the above items.

Next, let's try an exercise attributed to Warren Buffet:[9] write down a list of your top 25 career goals. Circle the five most important goals. Cross off the other 20 goals. Focus on the top five, break them down into steps, and pin them to the wall next to your desk where you'll look at them every day. Each week, revisit them and create another actionable step towards at least one of them. Evaluate how your daily activities are moving you towards or away from all five. This is a great focusing exercise to prevent you from getting sidetracked.

When you're starting out, you need to seek out where some people already share a common interest in what you are doing. When I started selling books at garden shows and craft fairs, the punk rock books were less popular so I had to bulk up on books about homemaking and food, but with the same edgy <u>cultural commentary</u>. I used different packaging

9 While Buffet has been widely credited with the creation of the exercise, he swears that it's not his, he doesn't use it, and can't speak to its merits either way. But think about it: maybe this exercise is one of the 20 things he crossed off of his list?

than the mainstream stuff, which seemed so boring to me. When we sell books at bicycle conferences, the number one question is "Are you a publisher who *only* publishes bicycle books?" We aren't but we can create that illusion because we've discovered that few people at these events have an interest in mental health titles or punk rock. When we sell books at peer mental health events, they want titles that go much deeper and only have a marginal interest in the bicycle and food titles. Yet, there is more crossover with punk. At roller derby events, there is interest in just about every topic we offer—except heterosexual sex books. You learn these things as you get more experienced and figure out what works and what doesn't.

W. Chan Kim and Renée Mauborgne created the concept of "Blue Ocean Strategy," which states that it's much cheaper and you are more likely to be successful doing business where you don't have competitors. You don't need to differentiate your efforts or establish demand when you're the only game in town. You'd be amazed how much uncontested space there is that will seem obvious once you take it over. For example, in 1996, I found it much easier to sell books in record shops and boutiques than in bookstores, because no one else was doing it. Today, that choice continues to form the backbone of the whole company, and others have started to use the oceans that we have "discovered." Our place within it is secure; most of the competition has since gone out of business. Rather than the rigidity of the mainstream, you create the norms and new demand for work like your own. When you have to come up with everything on your own, you come up with something original rather than attempting to compete in a crowded field where everyone else is better funded than you are.

Due to the highly competitive nature of grocery store shelf space, Jones Soda launched their drinks in skate park vending machines. This established an edgy reputation and ironic photography on their packaging. My neighbor is a roadside acupuncturist at long-distance cycling events. Food trucks at events are perhaps the best example of Blue Ocean Strategy. They improve the quality of the selection without having to face competitors or comparison pricing.

This is just the tip of the iceberg of marketing. Marketing is typically regarded as a dirty word. It means "telling people about things that could benefit them," but certainly, there's no shortage of dishonesty involved in its practices. For our purposes, please just think of it as "telling people how you have solutions for their problems." This simple act of connecting people to things has become much more complicated during an era where everyone feels overworked and has an endless array of shopping and entertainment options. I'll always think of the bookstore owner with a shop half a mile from a university campus who said "those kids aren't interested in what we do." When I asked "How have you reached out to them? Do they know how close you are?" he just stared at me and repeated "No, they aren't interested in books." Shatter all of your ill-conceived assumptions as you grow your sphere of awareness.

ETHICAL PRACTICE

The property next to our warehouse was previously used to create oils and gasses to process linoleum. The site had a series of buried tanks that inevitably leaked into the soil, causing decades of damage to our environment. When the building was bulldozed, the tanks weren't properly removed or decontaminated, making this everyone's problem—except the person who caused it.

These are the types of choices in business that we get to make every day. I had a restaurant boss who told me, "I would pour the fryer oil into the sewer if I didn't think the city would catch me." But most people who go into business do so because they have a strong vision for how they see the world differently. It's not (just) a matter of making more money. Most business owners work more hours than their salaried counterparts because they care not only about the impact of their work, but the work itself.

This is a great time to really think about *why* you are so motivated around your particular purpose. There's a great scene in *Parks and Recreation* where Tom is prepared to get an investor in a dry cleaning business only to suddenly abandon this plan in favor of his real passion: upscale, fine dining! Whether you care about serving high quality food or safe dry cleaning, this will fundamentally inform most of your decisions, including the wide parameters of what you are and are not willing to do, how to measure your own success, who you should hire, who your customers are, what you will outsource or handle yourself, and what your mission statement is.

Creating a mission statement may seem like a silly corporate exercise, but it is vital to keep you on track towards your goals. When you are small this is obvious and reflexive. I created Microcosm to create resources that were desperately lacking for me as a child to change the world around me and create a life where I wanted to be alive. From there, the choices are fairly obvious—at least to me. For other people it takes some explaining about who you are and who you are not, as an organization. If you can state your core work, values, and ethics in a pithy paragraph, then you can return to it anytime you need to explain to an employee, customer, partner, or yourself why you are or are not choosing to make any particular leap.

Part 2:

Strengthen What You Have

BUILD IT

*T*he number one mistake that small businesses make is that even after they have an employee or two, every action or decision must go through the owner. The primary leverage of having employees is not having to perform every job yourself. So if every paper towel purchase or customer sale requires consulting with the owner, you are setting yourself up for failure. Remember, each person only has a certain amount of capacity for information and decision making. Protect that treasure.

Instead, create systems for all aspects of your operation. What happens with deliveries? Whose responsibility are they? Create a series of checklists and flow charts for every task. These are often referred to as S.O.P.s, meaning standard operating procedures. They seem time consuming to create, and seem unnecessary when the business is still small, but trust the elders on this one. They are far easier to expand as you go, rather than create hastily when you desperately need them.

What happens when people arrive in the morning? Who is responsible for what? What are the triggers that signal when it's time to work down a checklist?

While most of our finances are automated by a database, I have monthly tasks of showing how we measured up against performance metrics to the staff. This means that I need to make sure all expenses have been uploaded before sharing a pie graph of how they break down. The staff has a right to know how sales and budgets are doing in regards to receiving bonuses. I break down sales by channel and where we have room to grow as well as areas that we should shrink or simplify. Sometimes—counterintuitively—lower sales with higher margins means that everyone can both perform less work and make more money.

As you fulfill items on each flow chart, evaluate ways to streamline them. How could they be made less cumbersome and more efficient? If I find that I have to remember to perform a certain task at irregular intervals, I add it to a biweekly checklist. Does it need done *now*? If not, next step! Do I have the best fundamental skills to be the one performing this task? If not, assign it to someone who does. If they make mistakes the first time, that's okay. Realign them to the goals of the task as you've defined them.

If they are still making the same mistakes after a few months, reassign it to someone else and take a closer look at their fundamental skills.

Your job is to make it clear—both in job descriptions and duties—who does what. Part of the system has to be reminding other people not to touch other people's duties, lest they do them incorrectly or put things in the wrong place where they are forgotten or lost. At Microcosm, we are constantly having to remind people to stay in their own lane. Yes, you could do that but it's someone's job. No, please do not post general requests to look for missing books, the inventory manager should look because she likely knows where it is, which is better than six people guessing or causing additional problems. Talking staff through how systems work is helpful because it shows them that they know just enough to cause problems but not enough to solve them. The more cooks that you put into the kitchen, the more you drive people away from their own stated goals. Think of people working in tandem rather than on the same task. I can assess how robust the systems of any organization are based on how focused each person is. Do they know what to do, what not to do, who to ask, when to ask, what sequence to handle their priorities in? This may seem small as you start out, but as you grow, having robust delegating systems is the fundamental difference between Henry Ford and the 502 competitors that were established before him.

In publishing, book development meetings typically involve editors, salespeople, the production department, and the bosses. The purpose of these meetings is to do product development—putting key language and imagery on the book cover that tells people what it is, what it isn't, who it's for, and who it's not for. But whenever these meetings contain more than three people, they devolve away from developing the marketing and into rabbit holes. "Wouldn't it be cool if this book was something else entirely?" or "I would be concerned that people outside of our demographic would be repelled by this book based on its themes." When doing product development, you need to maintain laser focus on the audience and their proclivities. You aren't concerned with theoretical or intellectual exercises. Left to their own devices, meetings can drive you away from your stated goals so it's vital to moderate them and remind people what your purpose is. Otherwise you could find fifteen minutes of back and forth whether the cover should be red or blue when the designer has long settled on yellow. People want to feel involved and invested in what is happening around them, so a better solution to maintain regular communication about decisions, changes, and each goal post that you reach and for that to always come from top management. This way people feel like you have it under control.

DON'T WATCH THE BEHEMOTH

Many companies are successful despite relentless, terrible decision making about how they run their business. If you read business news, you can literally read about major mistakes that companies like Apple, Coca Cola, Google, or Facebook make every single day. Yet these companies still exist. And they are growing. Why? Partially it's because of market dominance, but that took time. They did conquer their competitors, even if that happened a long time ago. Mostly it's because their proof of concept is remarkably sound. And a lot of it can be chalked up to being too big to fail. Our economy rewards behemoths. Worry about them as much as you would stare directly at the sun. You're only going to cause damage to yourself.

When I tell strangers that I work in book publishing, they recite headlines from the *New York Times*, mostly about Amazon, tell me how nobody reads anymore, and how digital has taken over. We can't run Microcosm like Amazon because we fundamentally lack the infrastructure, cashflow, or market dominance. OK, and the evilness.

This might sound like a weakness but it's a strength. While Amazon has convinced the public that publishers are obsolete and that nobody reads, the opposite is true. We are closer to the ground, we know our fans, what they love, what pisses them off, and what they've been seeking for years. What Amazon is doing is largely irrelevant for us. We're building our own platform, not latching onto theirs. This gives us much greater agency that isn't dependent on their decisions. Amazon, on the other hand, uses their products as a loss leader while only making money from cloud hosting and government contracts. Their long-term strategy appears to be losing money on sales until all of their competitors go out of business and then raising prices 3% each year. Could you afford to compete with that?

There are four factors that affect all businesses, regardless of size: money, people, tech, and globalization. Let's take a look at each one briefly while you think about how they affect big and small businesses in different ways.

Money

Most corporations with over 100 employees or who are traded on the public stock exchange operate with theoretical money. Meaning, they have enough trajectory and track record that they can borrow more money from someone new whenever their bank account is empty. Think of Donald Trump and bankruptcy. There's a certain inevitability to being born wealthy so think of these companies like the rich kid down the street, where it's easy to make $100,000 when you start with a million. Whereas smaller businesses have a line of credit or have to operate on an individual's actual money, with each day's deposit larger than its expenses. Neither one is better or worse, it's a matter of stakes and risk. While most people think that they need more capital or borrowing power, if big money is wielded wrong, it makes everything so much worse. Fundamentally, the needs are the same: you have to have financial underpinnings that make sense, earn more than you spend and don't drive faster than the car in front of you. You can create the illusion of success with a massive credied bt line, but you can't actually buy success in the long term—though you can certainly hire publicists to tell the press how successful you are until this claim is demonstrated to be false! Think Enron. For a while, it's easy to fabricate financial records, but when you are dealing in real money—and eventually you will be—even the best pyramid schemes fall apart.

People

The owner of our European distributor said that after 40 years, managing employees is the most difficult part of his business. What one person considers reasonable—and their justification for their behavior—is often patently absurd to the person they are explaining it to. Managing employees can be frustrating, but it's part of the human component of any organization. If you don't understand their behavior, customers, suppliers, and partners can appear even more confusing and fickle from a distance. A small business has a huge advantage here in that you can normally break this down into a civil conversation where someone will give you an honest answer without having to abide by miles of red tape from your employer to resolve a conflict. You can say "this is what isn't working for us, and this is the solution that we'd like to propose" and most people can negotiate that into a lasting, mutually beneficial resolution.

Technology

For 26 years, one of our most popular items has remained an annual planner. During the rise of the smartphone, sales dwindled. For a five year period, sales were cut in half, but 2020 was a record sales year for the planners. Consumers had found fatigue with the smartphone and paper was, in many ways, a superior solution for personal organization. Bigger companies and other industries have experienced much more devastating changes because of technology. Blockbuster Video was completely usurped by the rise of cloud computing and 85,000 people lost their jobs as a result. Netflix employs barely over 9,000 people because so much of the work is automated. The ramifications have hit far and deep, lowering the pay scale for filmmakers as well, while perpetuating the misleading idea of a level playing field. While Universal Music isn't the financial powerhouse that it was 30 years ago with the profitability of the compact disc, boutique bedroom record labels with limited pressings are finding tremendous demand for vinyl records. How has technology affected your industry?

Globalization

In 2008, President Obama reached out to Apple's CEO to ask what it would take for iPhones to be manufactured in U.S. factories. Obama was succumbing to pressure to restore domestic production after the U.S. had ceded most of its goods to be made in China over the past 30 years. China had invested heavily in manufacturing during this same period and had the immense population to support its factories. Apple explained that it wasn't a matter of cost so much as it was one of capacity: no U.S. facility had the ability to take all of those raw materials in a timely fashion and turn them around on the assembly line. The time and versatility of U.S. factories simply could not compare. During the COVID pandemic, however, we saw both of these systems tested. U.S. factories were desperately short on raw materials, workers, and transportation services while Chinese factories had the people and materials, but global supply chains were choked by excessive demand and it took four times as long for cargo to reach the United States at ten times the price. Consider how these factors will affect what you're doing. Even if you are making jewelry in your bedroom one piece at a time, it's very likely that you are reliant on materials from afar and that supply will ebb and flow.

What Problem Are You Solving?

The biggest mistake that you can make in business is to create something clever that utterly fails to solve a problem. Dean Kamen invented the Segway in 2001, long before the current scooter craze. Michael Milken invested heavily in it, with predictions that it would profit hundreds of millions and become as ubiquitous as the automobile. But unlike the scooter, the segway was a huge commercial failure. Why? There was no problem that needed solving. It didn't focus on any single user or demographic to evangelize for it. It was a variant on walking for people who wanted technology to step in. If Segway had focused on people with disabilities, the story might be different, but so would its development. The marketing team was not thinking about utility. With a sticker price of $3,000-7,000, they became a silly toy for rich people and the laughingstock for the rest of us. And they were dangerous: too fast for sidewalks, too slow and vulnerable for roads. $100 million was spent developing the final Segway yet few people found the value proposition enticing. The financial backer claimed that the Segway would replace the car and would set a record for how fast it reached one billion dollars in revenue. Some countries required motor vehicle licenses and others wouldn't let them use public roads at all. The segway never earned back 98% of that $100M development. The companies behind Bird and Lime scooters, on other hand, were immediately generating annual profits over $10M by inundating urban sidewalks, where the cost is a few dollars to rent for short trips and the vehicles offer a simple last mile transportation solution. Considering this contrast will give you a great new perspective on your own operations.

HOW TO GET SCALE

So you've got your solution to a real problem and your goals and your audience. You've established proof of concept. People want what you have. Now you just have to get it to scale without losing your shirt.

My mom had this incredible ability to look at something, identify its weakness, find a gray area in the rules, and exploit it for personal benefit. Through a lifetime of witnessing this, I learned how to evaluate an organization for a few minutes and identify key flaws. In one case, a membership organization which has been shrinking for years is forever in a budget crisis. Rather than taking a look at why members are leaving, making fundamental changes to plug the leak, recruiting back lost members and attracting new ones in the process, they raise prices to cover the budget deficit, continuing to scare away more and more legacy members. The trouble of any institutionalized thinking is that, well, you think like the organization that you've been acculturated into. You do the things that you've always done because "that's how we've *always* done things here. Duh!"

Or worse, you bring in new people and they want to bring with them the dysfunctional methods of their former employer, even one that went out of business.

So the first step is to evaluate your assumptions, be willing to let go of ingrained thinking, and walk through your process, checking where you are getting ahead and holding yourself back. This process can be painful and difficult because your responses are usually instinctive. So it can take some effort to ask yourself, "when I do this, what is the usual outcome? Is it what I am hoping for? Is it serving my goals?" Whenever Microcosm's sales double, old systems start to break down. Things that served us fine a year or two ago are totally dysfunctional because we are busier now. It takes a few months to notice this because this mental mapping is inherited from whatever you did before. That informs your thinking, just as your family of origin did and everything else that is hardwired into how you make each decision. It's hard to give up old ways because they used to work just fine for you. What informs your mental mapping?

To protect yourself from this pitfall, follow your established systems 75% of the time. This reduces your mental capacity load and makes things consistent and predictable for your co-workers. The other 25% of the time, after completing a task within the system, think critically about how that task could be streamlined more efficiently as you continue to grow. Test and revise accordingly. The magic is in knowing which time is appropriate for which. For your staff, adjust those numbers to 90/10% of the time. While it's primarily your job to incorporate systems into the big picture, your staff is closer to the ground and should inform your bird's eye view of where they think things can get tightened up. When considering your staff's feedback, you cannot just unilaterally adopt their ideas. Half of the time when their staff brings an issue to you, they are merely tired, frustrated, and complaining. Sometimes they merely cannot see how their ideas will negatively impact other staff. However, the other half of the time, the ideas that they bring you will be pure gold. Your job is to know which half of this feedback to implement.

Next, in order to hold a shared picture of the future you hope to create, you need to get everyone invested whose cooperation is necessary for your new mental map. Creating the path from here to there is called "systems thinking." The tendency of many small businesses is to go along with solutions that are offered to them or to react to the situations around them. If a customer is upset, it feels like a crisis, even if it's the first customer to have a problem in a month. But it feels more systemic because the other customers didn't contact you to express their eternal gratitude. For these reasons and better systems thinking, I have created the following infographic:

When I printed it on a poster for an employee who frequently had trouble with this aspect of her job, she declined it, citing that she had enough inspirational materials to decorate her workspace already. I tried to explain that this was training and an exercise to do her job better, but a cultural disconnect was brewing. She continued to do things her own way and when I explained why this was a problem, instead of taking this feedback, she attempted to justify her actions and create her own policies. Her approach to her job was making it unnecessarily complicated and driving us away from our prime directives. Because she thought that she knew better and could set her own company priorities, I call this archetype "The Rogue." For example, it can feel like a valid argument for an employee to insist that customer service should be prioritized above all else, but one rogue agent like

How to Make a Decision

What is my desired outcome?

What is the simplest solution to achieve it? Is there an easier way?

Does my idea work for everybody involved?

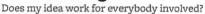 Y / N

Are the costs & consequences acceptable?

 Y / N

What are the worst, best, and likely outcomes? Can I manage them all?

 Y / N

Does this decision cause harm to anyone I care about and/or our relationship?

 Y / N

Does this decision take too much time and energy
from the things I want and need to do?

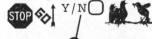 Y / N

Could this decision cost more money than I can afford? Is there a cheaper way?

 Y / N

DO IT!

this almost always undermines your prime directive and it only results in increasing amounts of conflict because they are often playing against the rest of their team.

One of the fundamental aspects of a team is that you need to be working together within the systems. Otherwise, your efforts can't form a sum greater than its parts.

LEVERAGE

Without breaking a sweat, even the least fit person can bicycle past a jogger who spent months or years honing their body into powerful, athletic shape. Why? The bicycle, the simplest of machines, provides so much leverage that it transforms a tiny amount of exertion through gears that make each of your muscle movements more powerful. Your business should work the same way.

There are lots of things that I fill my time with as a CEO. Principally, my metric is that any activity that I do on the clock has to either be something that I greatly enjoy or something where the future income is at least $1,000/hour from that activity, usually more. This means that while I do vacuum the break room because I like to see it clean, most of my time is spent negotiating contracts, selling rights to create audiobooks of our titles, signing off for salespeople to establish special terms for a new wholesaler, determining why certain titles aren't available in certain countries, talking to the freight company who sent the last nine shipments to the wrong warehouse and convincing our partners to change shippers, and analyzing the data to see what to add, where to grow, and how to get there most easily.

These things felt amorphous or "extra" for years, but now I see that they're the best use of my time. There are other people who pack orders, manage our employees directly, or correct something that is billed incorrectly. While I enjoy making sure that orders fluidly move out the door, the people who handle that are top notch. And it is a much more valuable use of my time to look at patterns, make predictions, and use this information to plan our rosiest future because these are skills that others don't possess to the same degree that I do.

Similarly, you need to leverage your employees. I once met a business owner who said that he fired all of his staff because he looked at the numbers, what wealth they produced, and what he paid them and decided that they weren't worth the hassle. His assessment was incomplete. The problem was that he didn't know how to leverage his staff and instead of learning how, he shrank his operation. Leveraging your employees is your job, not theirs, but it is its own skill set. Obviously, there's nothing wrong with downsizing and some owners are happier as a one person shop, but it has its limitations, notably lack of growth.

As an owner, if you don't enjoy doing something or someone else could perform a task just as well as you do or even more effectively than you can, delegate it. Gradually, you should be refining your task list down to two categories:

- Things that are **urgent**: the clock is ticking and if you wait too long, you will lose your chance. E.g., you need to plan for an event this weekend or a pallet of inventory is about to be shipped to the wrong address.

- Things that are **important**: there is a large reward at stake. E.g., your biggest customer from last year says that they are interested in a selection of new offerings or someone important that you met at a trade show expressed an interest in working together, giving you their card. Running your end of month data report is important, because it will *hopefully* change how you make future decisions.

As the owner, you should always be focusing on one of these two types of tasks. Sometimes this does mean doing menial work after everyone else has gone home on Friday because something needs to happen, but that means that task is *urgent*.

At any given moment, the next task that you should do is the one that is both the most urgent and has the greatest benefit. If you are understaffed, that's proceeding through steps to hire more people. If you have someone inquiring about a deal that could double the number of people that your work reaches, you should think critically about their claims and how realistic they are, then get in touch. The task with the greatest leverage isn't always about a guaranteed outcome. Often you have to explore some trails that dry up after a few minutes, days, weeks, or years. Sometimes even a spam email can be a goldmine, though most are not worth the second it takes to delete them. Even when the government is unreasonable, they are one vendor that you can never ignore or disregard. Even if you only owe $58 in sales tax, they will escalate fees and seizures until you pay, so go ahead and create a workflow to make sure that the government never has to call you first. Once that's out of the way, if a service provider could reduce your expenses by $80,000 every year while simultaneously expanding your reach 20% via new online platforms, it's worth at least having a conversation with them to make sure that what they offer is legal and would work for you. However, there's nothing urgent about those things if you are currently struggling to make payroll: you need to figure out how to get some money in your account. Focus both on the next possible disaster you can prevent and the next goal that you'd like to accomplish. Make tangible steps for each and figure out which one has the greatest leverage in the long term.

A common side effect of the pressure and stress of ownership is putting off tasks that are "difficult." Preparing for a job interview candidate, filing sales tax for the first time, or setting up worker's comp insurance can all feel monumental...and thus it's common to decide "let's just stick with something easier today." Oddly enough, you'll almost always see that your dread has built the task up in your mind, and when you do it, it's actually within your abilities and skills. The term "time blindness" is often associated with ADHD, but applies to a shocking amount of the general population. It means that you think a five minute task will take hours and shelve it as weeks and months pass you by on the calendar, neglecting something that you could have finished long ago. Conversely, you'll get better at predicting how complicated "easy" tasks are and stop being a week late to dinner! So face your fears, don't delay the "difficult" tasks, and quickly you'll build up your confidence by finding that you can literally do anything!

When you assign a task to someone, look at the outcome of that task. What is it producing? The simplest metric for this is thinking of two workstations, side by side. One employee packs 100 orders per hour with 99% accuracy. The other packs 62 orders per hour and only has 82% accuracy. What usually happens in this scenario is that the first employee finishes their tasks halfway through the day and looks like a slacker to their boss while the second can successfully fly under the radar as "normal." So what tends to happen is that the higher performing employee gets frequent lectures about how they need to look busy and probably goes to work somewhere else. In reality, balancing and assigning workload is the manager's job. That person simply needs more work to do and probably to be promoted with greater responsibilities. You need to reward someone exceeding your expectations rather than holding them at a lower level than their capabilities.

A person who understands the leverage of that task and cares to do it correctly can often oversee others doing it. This is much more valuable than merely performing that task. Even after giving that person a raise, everyone benefits. Similarly, we hired someone to pack orders, who began pointing out ways to her boss that the system could be streamlined, automated, and made more efficient. Now, a bad boss would grudgingly listen, explain why it was impossible, make a note that she complained, and send her to pack more boxes. What this actually reveals is that she excels at systems thinking, was performing beyond her pay grade and that we should give her more responsibilities. Many of her ideas were adopted by our software coding department to eliminate errors and time-consuming tasks. She is now a vital conduit between these two departments and we gave her a raise.

Evaluate every task that you do, how it could be more efficient, and what the ultimate outcome of it is. The longer that one person has done it in isolation, the more likely that systems thinking or technology could allow that person to find higher leverage tasks.

When the rogue who refused the "How to make a decision" poster left, her managers took a look at her job duties, performance metrics, and her approach to achieving them. For each task, she would spend hours taking the data from our native systems and populating it into external communication software. She would then train interns and delegate her work to them. She would arrange meetings that didn't have leverage, and her performance metrics continually failed to meet her manager's needs or expectations. She had effectively created a way to make ten hours of work into a full time job. So when she left, instead of hiring a replacement, we reorganized the job duties of three people and gave the entire staff a 7% raise.

ALIGN THE VALUE CHAIN

Remember, everything in business is about aligning systems so that they work fluidly without intervention. A bad owner thinks in terms of punishments and rewards. A good owner aligns systems to incentivize desired behavior. The distinction seems small if it's a new concept but the difference is immense. The simplest way to accomplish this is making your own best interest the same as the customer's, the supplier's, and your employees'.

Think of the carrot as aligning upstream and downstream incentives. You have something that your customer wants, your supplier wants to sell to you, and your employees get a bonus when they exceed performance metrics. Seems obvious, right? Evaluate and remove barriers to create the desired outcome. If customers want to talk to a live person instead of a phone system, have a live person answer your phone. If retailers put your product into square boxes when it arrives, do that at the factory. This is called "vertical incentive alignment."

Think of the stick as a strategic control point, a market that can be leveraged for superior margins because one party controls it. In our case, Microcosm sells to about 3,000 stores, most of which buy all of their books from us. So in this way, suppliers are inclined to be distributed by us because there is no other way to be sold into those stores. This situation aligns the carrot and the stick. Suppliers want to work with us. We supply something that the stores want on their shelves. Our employees benefit because when our bottom line is paid for each month, they begin accruing bonuses. By keeping the carrot and stick aligned our continued growth is relatively assured.

On the other hand, similar to the Blue Ocean Strategy, the vast majority of our retailers buy all of their books from us. if our primary market was selling to bookstores, the discounts and payment schedules of each sale would be dictated to us and we'd have much more competition for shelf space. Most publishers that I talk to still assume that most books are sold on Amazon. Publishers bend over backwards to accommodate Amazon, Amazon dictates all terms of the sale, publishers find the sales underwhelming, and worst of all—the cash flow is insufficient to cover the costs of production and operation.

Your organization's value chain is everything that goes into making your final service or product. For example, books begin as farm trees in China and the United States. Trees are turned into paper in mills. Distributors sell this raw material to printers, who also handle printing and binding. Authors submit manuscript pitches to our office and we evaluate, based on marketability, which ones to publish. We edit, design, and market these books and send them to our printer. These bound books are boxed and shipped to our warehouse in Cleveland. Salespeople maintain relationships with retailers and our staff ship finished books to stores and wholesalers. Unsold books are returned to us for credit. We collect payment from customers and attempt to solicit restock orders every few months. Unsold books are sold for pennies on the dollar to remainder firms and books that cannot be sold in this fashion are recycled back into paper pulp and made into new books. Millions of books are recycled and 24% of new books are printed on post-consumer paper.

Control points are anywhere during your value chain where every industry participant is heavily reliant on a single product, solution, or service. In the book publishing industry, some examples would be freighting—especially from China during the holiday season—or paper mills, which are heavily regulated by the U.S. federal government. So many book printers went out of business over the past fifteen years that when interest in books grew in 2020, there was not enough paper or printers. When there is a shortage, the entire industry suffers because we do not have alternatives and need to find creative solutions or lean heavily on personal relationships instead. Similarly, most book publishers choose from only a small handful of trade distributors, so the quality of these services is not very competitive and publishers consider themselves lucky to have a distributor at all. Most publishers market to the same 2,500 bookstores in the U.S. and find that this shelf space is incredibly competitive when the stores have fifteen million or so books to choose from! For this limited shelf space, there is much greater supply than demand.

Evaluate your own value chain and control points. For example, every smartphone manufacturer is heavily reliant on coltan, a mineral mined mostly in Africa. This allows the coltan mines to set the prices and manufacturers to be happy to purchase any at all. Of course, the power in this relationship could switch if coltan could be replaced in electronics with a synthetic, the same way that rubber harvesting was impacted during the 1970s.

In the 1990s, it seemed like folly for Apple to again challenge the market dominance of Microsoft, but Apple created more robust hardware and software and took computers from the realm of nerds to the mainstream. As Microsoft created clunkier and clunkier user interfaces and less robust operation systems, Apple created sleek designs and smooth user interfaces. Apple literally made computers hip! Who controls the power in your industry? How could you change or step around that?

Make a list of all of the activities that you have to perform to do business. Look at who controls these activities. For example, it doesn't make sense to start a company that manufactures laser printers. The market is dominated by household names that sell printers at a loss to capitalize later on toner sales. You simply couldn't compete. You would have to invent a new kind of printer that revolutionizes that market and makes your competitors obsolete, scrambling to catch up to you. Even then, how would you reach your future evangelists?

Vertical integration is when a company handles an aspect of their business that would normally be handled by an outside company, like a publisher handling printing. You might have read about Delta Airlines buying an oil refinery in 2012 to make their own fuel. The difference in cost between crude oil and refined jet fuel fluctuates wildly, so the move made sense. Still, many experts were dubious because vertical integration is very hard to do well, and, in the end, the results varied for Delta. Direct sourcing is a good idea when a market is unstable, like oil can be from time to time. In my 2019 book, *A People's Guide to Publishing*, I wrote "it almost never makes sense for any publisher to finance and learn to operate printing equipment." My opinion was completely changed the following year by the pandemic.

During the COVID pandemic, just about every manufacturer in any field was dependent on raw materials that were in incredibly short supply. In the U.S. there weren't enough mills turning trees into rolls of paper because the expectation was that demand would plummet. Instead, paper prices increased and turnaround times for printing books tripled. For the first time in decades, there weren't enough book printers so they could effectively set the terms of every transaction.

In the same way, restaurants are expected to have Coke or Pepsi products. While this watered-down version of sugar is arguably the inferior version of Coke or Pepsi's bottled drinks, customers are going to be confused and annoyed if your restaurant doesn't offer them because it's simply *standard*. For the same reason, if you are launching a new soft drink company, restaurants aren't going to be a great pipeline to consumers.

Since all of our books are produced by the thousands, one problem we have is that customers feel like they can simply buy them later. In real time, scarcity begets immediacy. This is why limited editions are so popular in the modern era. Mass-produced items create a paradox where there is no immediacy to buy. We often have people walk up, browse, and say "Okay, maybe I'll be back" which essentially means "I feel no urgency in buying." We created a page on our website that contains only books with one copy left and it immediately increased sales of those titles by over 2000% because it connects the carrot and the stick of "if you don't buy, you may never get to." It lights a bit of a fire and makes people decide if they want something or not.

For every decision that you make, list every available option. Draw a branch for each strategic move. Then list every option your supplier or competitors might take in response. Assess the outcome of each competitor's move with probabilities and weights. Then, pick the best outcomes for you. Remember, you don't want to create an adversarial relationship with your own suppliers or staff. The relationships need to be mutually beneficial.

NEVER DRIVE FASTER THAN THE CAR IN FRONT OF YOU

Remember the need to respect what is going on around you? You do not and will not ever exist in a bubble, especially when it feels like it. Consider your positioning in relation to your environment. Who are your competitors? What are they doing? What are they *not* doing? Why not? What gaps are they leaving for you in your market? Why aren't they going after these gaps? Are they oblivious or are these gaps a pain in the ass to service? What will likely change in the next year? Five years? Ten years? By paying attention to your environment and not operating in isolation, you'll be much better at predicting these forces, instead of reacting to changes at pinch points or the eleventh hour. For example, if you're just now signing a book about a zombie love story when that trend is saturated and peaking, it's likely that you'll be met with malaise and your books will be sold for scrap on the bargain rack by the time it's published two years later. For some businesses, this means that it's better to avoid trends altogether. For others, they are adept at riding the wave of a trend and hopping onto the next one just before the wave crashes. Know your skillset. And build your relationships accordingly.

ALWAYS NEGOTIATE

*I*f you place an agreement in front of the vast majority of the U.S. population, they will sign it without thinking. A notable portion will even sign it without even *reading* it. The reality is that while most agreements aren't exploitative, they do have key areas of wiggle room that ultimately helps the agreement hold up and serve both parties better over time.

The goal of negotiating is to create an agreement that will continue to work for both parties for as long as possible. If you twist the agreement so far in your favor, the other party will terminate it at their earliest possible opportunity. If the agreement doesn't actually work for you, you will be forced to decide whether to end it or attempt to maintain a pleasant attitude through bad choices that you made—or complain endlessly about how the choices that you made put you in a compromised position.

Negotiating an agreement isn't just about upholding your own relative worth, though that's certainly a vital part of it. You have to look at what you have to offer, why the other party is making this agreement with you and what *they* have to gain from it. If you undervalue yourself, you will get stomped all over because you consented to something that doesn't serve your true worth. If you overvalue your worth, the other party will likely scoff once they see the agreement in practice for a while and end it when they can.

One of the biggest mistakes that I see managers make is that once money is coming in, they start spending freely. They look at their bank account and say "Yes, I can afford that." They aren't evaluating the benefits of each dollar spent and what it is accomplishing for them. There are innumerable benefits of always keeping costs down, but let's look at the most important ones:

- You can evaluate the benefits of how each decision works in practice and expand on the ones that are working while retracting from the ones that don't.

- As new opportunities present themselves, you aren't trapped by having spent your money.

- As the environment and factors change, you can react and adapt to things outside of your control.

If you aren't always keeping costs down, you are limiting your future choices because you don't yet know how you are compromising yourself. Always compare costs and benefits and remind yourself what your goals are. Remember that painful mantra from my years of doing consulting work, "...but we've always done things this way?" Well, it affects new businesses too. Brains have this strange propensity to notice how others conduct themselves, frame this as "the only way to do things" and to mimic these methods. In reality, the best solution to any problem is almost always the creative one that nobody else has thought of. This benefits everyone because it removes you from being in an adversarial relationship with the other parties that you are negotiating with and solving the problem elsewhere. For example, when the city refused to negotiate with us about adding to our warehouse, we made use of a zoning exception where you can add storage units on your property without a permit. So we built five of them. Similarly, when dividing up sales territories, I was happy to give the traditional ones to the experienced sales rep groups—because I had created new markets for books that nobody else was reaching. We weren't at odds; their sales were the icing on the cake.

Familiarize yourself with what is standard in any agreements that you make. Don't ask for changes simply to see if they are granted, but it's okay to ask "Our other vendor provides an additional 30 days to pay and doesn't charge us credit card processing fees. Would that be possible?" They may flatly refuse, either because they simply cannot afford to do those things or because the person that you are negotiating with may not have permission to grant it.

Even if an agreement is fundamentally exploitative, it's unhelpful to inform the other party of this fact. They either already know and don't care or they need things to be this way or have some flexibility. Instead, it's much more helpful to say "Would it be possible to shorten the duration to one year with all rights reverting back to me, even if we continue working together?" This way, you're opening a conversation instead of closing a door. You are finding out more information that may change the terms of the discussion. If what you ask for isn't possible, they can access a window into your hesitations and create a counteroffer that might suit you even better! Seeing how they behave during the negotiation sometimes saves you from painful years of working together!

In some cases, the agreements that you make when you begin an agreement will be intractably enforced for many years so it's important to make sure that the best, worst, and most likely scenarios work for you under those agreements. Another reasonable question is "Can we revisit this next quarter and see if there's wiggle room on these matters based on how this agreement is working in practice?"

If a new agreement or relationship *could* work for you but you can get better service elsewhere, sometimes the best thing that you can do is to politely turn them down but suggest that the door is always open if they want to ask again later. This communicates not only the refusal but that they would need to sweeten the pot or for broader circumstances to change. For example, when the labor and paper shortages swept the publishing industry in 2020, we needed as many vendors as we could muster. I had to put my tail between my legs and reapproached many printers that I intended to never work with again. The world changes, so don't close any doors. What doesn't make sense today likely will in five years. Or at least, you cannot predict what your needs will be at that time. So there's no point in making enemies out of salespeople.

SAY YES AND NO

One of the hardest things about being a business owner is figuring out what you want to do and what you don't want to do. Something even harder than that is communicating those yeses, nos, and maybes effectively.

And if you remember nothing else about this section, remember this: *Clear is kind.*

Joe and Faith have been both employees and employers. You have almost certainly been an employee, and perhaps have also been an employer. So you know how frustrating it is to work with people who can't just say *what the hell is going on.* Maybe they don't know how to set a boundary, maybe they don't want to be seen as bad guys. But *fuck*, just tell me "yes" or "no" or "I have no fucking idea, let me get back to you." And while not wanting to be hurtful is a valid goal for anyone to have, sighing and beating around the bush because you don't want to disappoint someone isn't actually helpful. By avoiding communicating something to prevent letting someone down, *we almost always let them down more.*

And being able to say "no" to things you do want to do, not just the things you don't want to do, is powerfully important to your success. Imagine a customer wants their product delivered by EOD Wednesday. You know you could get it done by Friday, but there is a very good chance you wouldn't be able to make Wednesday happen without some shoddy work. You also *really* want this happy and returning customer. You think, *I can push through and make Wednesday happen.* Maybe you succeed or maybe you miss the mark, but *either way* you have created a problem. If you fail, you lose a customer in an epic way by overpromising. If you succeed, you have set up a dynamic with this customer that you will jump through hoops if they tell you to. *Forever.* Neither is good for the health of your business, your employees, or you.

What happens, instead, if you say, *"I would love to make that deliverable date for you. However, I value you as a customer too much to try to do so and fail in that expectation. I know I can have it done by Friday, and can commit to that. And I understand that if Wednesday is a hard limit for you, you will need to go somewhere else, but hopefully we can work together in the future."*

What happens, instead, if an employee you adore is struggling financially, is asking for a raise you would love to be able to give them and cannot at the moment? Same thing, right? What if you say *"I value you so much as an employee and your request for a raise is an entirely reasonable one. I'm working on building to a place where I can better compensate you for the work you do, and you will absolutely get a salary increase before I do. But I don't anticipate being able to do that until next year. If you can't wait and need to find a different job, I entirely understand and will give you the best reference anyone has ever seen. But if there is something we can do to help keep you here, let's talk about that. Do you need to flex out your schedule mid-afternoon to pick up your kiddo from school? I'm fine with them doing their homework here while you finish your day if that saves you money on afterschool care."*

By staying honest and congruent with your reality, you can better explain how you arrived at these solutions and where you can be flexible both now and in the future. Perhaps even more important, if the situation worsens and the other party behaves badly, you'll have a solid track record and reputation of communicating positively, and this will be remembered and recognized over time.

PERSPECTIVE

One of the most difficult lessons to learn is perspective. Both on how others see the world and your own clearest vision on your life. No matter how good or bad things are going, you will *always* have a "biggest problem." Sometimes it's that you are going out of business, but most days it's just that someone is doing something irritating that might eventually cause a bigger problem, or you can't figure out a weird document that you received. Keeping your head on straight about these things can be one of the most difficult aspects of running a business. Because it always *feels* like something is *terribly* wrong. Stress has a way of misleading your brain about the severity of your problems and causing further anxiety, to make you consider things that aren't *yet* problems but *might* be!

Faith has looked at the research on perspective-taking, and it shows that it is incredibly difficult for humans to do, and we rarely do it naturally. But it also shows that if we train ourselves to be better at it, the benefits are outstanding in terms of helping us tolerate distress and strengthen our capacity for empathy.

Perspective-taking is a metacognitive task. Metacognition is when the mind (our us-ness) recognizes what the brain is up to. The mind is self-aware, the brain isn't. So think of perspective-taking as a conscious, stagewise process so you habituate yourself to it.

1) What are you focusing on? Your own sense of overwhelm? The behavior of an employee? Get specific.

2) What are you noticing? Come up with as many possibilities as possible. Which seems most likely? For example, if you are feeling overwhelmed with deliverables and afraid of failure, what might the mechanism behind that feeling be? Because you were often called a failure when you were growing up? What buttons are being pushed?

3) Now, don't overly attach to that hypothesis, but follow it with curiosity. Does it hold up when you bear witness to how you are interacting with the world? Does it follow when you observe your own thoughts and feelings?

4) Now let's get a little CBT-ish[10] with it. Is your reactivity based in reality? And even if so, are you negotiating with yourself in a helpful way? Maybe you aren't meeting your projected goal for the quarter...is calling yourself a failure helpful? Not in the least. Telling yourself "I didn't set out to do what I intended....so here is my chance to learn from this experience to either hit my targets in the future or move them to something more readily achievable."

5) Make your decisions based on this more balanced thinking. You don't have to throw everything into the chuck-it bucket because you're in a bad spot at this particular moment. Is what you are doing still better than working for someone else? Even if you are delivering pizzas as a side hustle in the evenings to make payroll. Or is this not the thing and you need to reevaluate this business as a viable entity? We're not trying to convince you to stay on a sinking ship, we just hope you will make

---

10 CBT is short for Cognitive Behavioral Therapy, a hugely popular evidenced based practice in which the focus is on how your thoughts and feelings influence your behavior. It helps you unpack your automatic thoughts, rules about the world, and core beliefs so you can reframe situations in order to respond more effectively.

decisions from a place of recognizing as many of the moving parts as possible so you have fewer regrets later.

As you get more comfortable with these steps, take a daily inventory. What is the worst thing that could happen as a result of this? How are you planning ahead? How can you resolve this in the simplest manner? Quickly, as you develop more experience, you can learn to manage stress and anxiety better through a better relationship with perspective.

At the end of the day, you have to weigh the stress of working for yourself against that of having a job. And usually—pretty quickly—when you compare running a business against the worst aspects of having a job—all of that stress washes away.

EVALUATION

I would assume that the most common question that I would receive about business is "How do I know if I'm winning?" but most people aren't thinking this way. What people actually ask is "What can I do now that things aren't working out as I had hoped?" So I'd suggest that you can get ahead of both questions by creating metrics to know the answers at any given time.

Success, however, is a much more nebulous definition. What do you ultimately want to achieve? How do you measure that you are achieving it? What is it that brought you into business in the first place? Do you want to grow to a certain size and then stop growing or sell the company to someone else? What motivates you on a daily basis?

In most cases, you know if you are winning because you are growing 5-20% per year. At this rate of growth, it demonstrates that people are interested in what you are doing, your systems can grow and scale, that you can finance this growth realistically without it breaking you, and that your concept was good to begin with. And most importantly, at this rate of growth, you won't burn yourself out or throw up your hands at the impossibility of your definition of success.

You need to be collecting and evaluating your data. You need to know what you're looking at and what it means. A simple thing to do when you're starting out is to create a spreadsheet. Plug any metric that you can measure onto it, everything from monthly sales to inventory levels to expenses. As you keep records of these, start dividing this year's figure by last year's and last year's by the year before. Then take notice of patterns. Is your income growing proportionately with your payroll costs? What expenses are growing faster than your sales? In what ways are you planning for the future? In what ways could you plan better?

We sort our expenses in the same categories as our taxes and sort our income by as many categories as we can. This way it reveals the maximum amount of transparency as you drill down deeper into your data. This is to look at *which* areas of your operation are working as well as where you need to spend less.

As you grow, you need to maintain some checks and controls. How do you know that you are doing well? What are signs that suggest caution? How are you measuring up against short- and long-term goals? What tasks are falling behind or to the wayside? What is no longer necessary? Which tasks need to be delegated? When should you hire another person? When do you *need* to hire another person? What should that person be doing? How do you set larger strategic goals? You can determine answers to all of these questions and so much more by accumulating, spending time with, and becoming comfortable with your own data.

You can use your accumulated data with your spreadsheets to predict the future. Look at the changes from this year to last year and apply that same percentage difference to the following months. It won't be perfect, but you can effectively estimate a safe approximation of what will happen based on the current trajectory.

Similarly, if you add up all of your expenses and compare to your future income estimates, you can estimate your future cash flow. You know when bills are due. You know how much money you have now and you can estimate how much you will make next month. You can see when you'll run out of money and when you'll have money to afford to hire another person or give out bonuses. Unlike a business plan, these numbers become increasingly concrete, and it can be shocking how accurate they are. Think about new ways to use this information to create new systems. Looking into the future and growth ideas, you can determine what you could accomplish through borrowing money and if the cost of doing so would outweigh the benefits. Creating more and more data sets, metrics, and evaluation systems is the best way to consider and make any decision.

The most important thing about having systems is putting checks and balances on them and revisiting both weekly or monthly. Sometimes the answers are obvious. When we sold coffee at our bookstore, it didn't work out because we didn't open until 11 AM. If you have a hair salon and shift your open hours two hours later each day, how would this affect your income? How do your best customers feel about this? Be willing to experiment but know when to throw in a towel and switch back.

Through experimentation, you'll quickly see what people are more responsive to and, often, customers are enthusiastic that you are willing to experiment because it shows that you are open to suggestions. You'll discover that sometimes very small changes can create exponential growth.

Sometimes raising your prices makes you appealing to an entirely different type of customer—for the very same services. A graphic design firm told me that their most difficult jobs were consistently the customers on the lowest end of their sliding scale pricing. With costs so low, the customers didn't plan ahead to develop a strong idea of what they wanted, effectively creating more work and revisions for the design firm. By raising prices, the same customers became less hassle because they took the costs and time invested more seriously.

Once you get a good rhythm and groove established, you'll begin to know instinctively how and when to grow. But until then, growth is best by doubling down on what you are good at. If you have a series of laundromats that are wildly accumulating quarters, open more laundromats. Don't try to open a bar. It's a different kind of business. Our 2021 sales grew 115% over 2020, which grew 68% over 2019. We reached the point where it simply wasn't possible to store and retrieve inventory or have enough people working at the same time. We had to add an additional warehouse. We doubled our fulfillment staff and warehousing capacity but we waited too long to do so. We weren't confident that the growth would sustain. We doubted the math. It was a serious folly. Never doubt the math. It helps you better predict and prepare for the future. Take a look at your current trajectory and assess when you will no longer be able to sustain it from a lack of staff and infrastructure.

Some people love borrowing money and taking chances, but I like to grow my own success organically and fund my growth from prior sales. This isn't always possible and there are definitely times to borrow money, but you can assess your own comfort level with various risks. The one thing that is certain is that you want to be firmly confident in your idea of how to expand before you take any chances.

To determine if an idea is a good one, use the return on investment calculation: net income / (property + (assets - liabilities)). This shows you what the best uses of your effort are, based on your costs and outcomes. By comparing two different options that you are considering, this formula can see what the opportunity cost is on this particular activity. For example, you can look at the costs of opening an additional restaurant versus moving into a different location. You can compare adding a new product line versus adding an additional fulfillment center. Again, this stuff can feel confusing and cumbersome, but as you get more comfortable with it, it's a great way to make decisions. Combining it with your knowledge of your industry can be game changing.

Sometimes the best thing that you can do is to set a more ambitious goal. Once upon a time it seemed outrageous to hope for $1 million in annual book sales but today we sell in a day what we used to in a month. We open more new accounts per month than we used to all year. Often, the problem is simply aiming too low. And you'll see how aiming higher informs all of your other decisions.

Once you reach your current goal, establish a bigger one. This way you are never resting on your laurels but always evaluating what you are doing right and wrong. You won't reach unbridled growth forever, but if you cease having aspirations, you'll stop expanding as well. Sure, it can feel fun to occupy a comfortable and familiar niche. But, usually these thoughts and feelings are prompted by fears of the unknown. So embrace and get comfortable with your feelings so that you can work through them. Similarly, sometimes your next step is a matter of determining which actions not to repeat. Overcoming cultural habits within your organization can be a lodestone.

Don't be one of the many companies who hire me to consult for them but don't want to change anything.

KNOW WHEN TO QUIT

Sometimes, it's not you, it's them. For decades, Blockbuster could rent the same movie over and over from thousands of strip mall locations. But this business model was disrupted when online streaming usurped the market and Blockbuster passed when given the opportunity to buy Netflix. Quickly, direct-to-consumer modeling took over, as the same companies who made the movies could distribute them to customers. Blockbuster's annual revenues declined as its debt-to-equity ratio—the amount of money owed divided by the value of property—skyrocketed. In short, the world had changed, but Blockbuster had not. It was time to quit.

A friend's parent's company was bleeding money on a much smaller level. They sold pre-digital office equipment and had a host of dedicated customers that they felt loyal to. But each year their debts went up because there simply wasn't need for what they did any longer. Rather than throw in the towel, they mortgaged the house and downsized their warehouse. Before long, the debts kept climbing because they weren't fixing the fundamental problem. My friend had to come home and shut down his parent's business.

It's pretty simple. You'll know that it's time to quit if you continue to have to borrow money despite the fact that your company is not growing. There's a time and a place for financing being helpful, but if you continue to need to borrow despite having functional systems in place, something isn't working. It's time to look under the hood, see where all of this money is going, and determine if you can make changes or you are simply losing money on each sale.

Similarly, sometimes after years of long hours you'll simply be burned out. The business works just fine but maybe it's time for you to find someone else to grab the reins—temporarily or permanently. That's okay too. It's about being honest with yourself.

Part 3:

Build Your Skills and Team

f your systems, ideas, and concept are sound, you'll soon find yourself with the opposite problem: your business just keeps growing. And you need to constantly learn new things and hire more people because you can't do everything yourself. Let's take a look at how to achieve that.

STAGNATING LEADERS

Power comes from authority

Privatizes information

Discourages team from developing ideas

Dictates solutions to problems

Minimizes time & resources for problem solving

Believes in strict roles & responsibilities

Deals reactively to problems

Reviews staff performance once per year

EFFECTIVE LEADERS

Power comes from collaboration

Shares information

Encourages suggestions and ideas

Collectivizes solutions to problems

Allocates time and resources to prevent problems

Roles and responsibilities are fluid and evolve

Resolves root causes of problems

Provides immediate and ongoing feedback and personalized coaching

PEOPLE MANAGEMENT

As you grow, hire people that are smarter than you are and better at a specific job. It can be a job that you don't enjoy or excel at or one where it's better to have a specialist. It can feel threatening to hire someone that you can see is smarter than you, but fundamentally that's who you want on your team. I am skilled at production management, product development, financial management, and data analytics so my partners handle editorial, marketing, publicity, customer service, human resources, sales, fulfillment, and people skills. You will always have your own skills and value and you are merely building from there to create something more robust by supplementing your own strengths. Smart people make smart decisions and can be great foils for refining your good ideas into great ideas.

Once your organization is larger than yourself, you need to really think about your team culture. If you complain all the time and find the negative aspects of everything, you'll quickly see that your employees do too. If complaining about customers'

relatively mundane and reasonable requests is the flavor of the month, you'll see it repeated rampantly. If small problems are cavorted around like the sky is falling, you'll see that your staff will carry themes of doom and gloom about the future of their job.

It's for these reasons that you want to be conscious and deliberate about your team culture. Listen to people. Most employees (or customers) who make unreasonable demands don't actually expect you to accommodate them. They want to feel like you listen to their concerns and that you care. As relationships and trust form, you want these things to extend to the top so that people feel comfortable coming to you with their problems, knowing that you'll take them seriously. Otherwise, frustrations and grievances will fester and you will often not know what is upsetting the people that you need to work closely with because they don't feel comfortable telling you.

While it will feel excessive, like you are too busy, or even sometimes like a waste of time, meet for ten minutes each week with each of your staff that reports directly to you. When you have managers, have their staff report to them for ten minutes each week as well. This keeps lines of communication open and gives an intentional space to resolve problems and grievances before they fester. In these meetings, first answer anything each report needs information about, then discuss any projects they are working on but haven't been able to finish since last week and why, then discuss what they have accomplished. Offer ongoing performance feedback so that each person knows where they stand in relation to their goals and management's perspective. You want everyone to have a very clear picture of what they need to do to achieve their personal goals. By discussing matters in this sequence it shifts the focus and sets the tone that you are creating the expectation of accomplishing tasks and overcoming hurdles. It's a manager's job to make their employees' lives easier, not the other way around.

In a hierarchical management arrangement, there is extreme rigidity and almost no room for any individual decision making, people are treated as interchangeable units that are easily replaced, and systems are exceptionally unforgiving. Examples of this would be Starbucks or McDonald's, where Henry Ford would be jealous of the lengths that they have improved upon his invention of the assembly line. There are obvious downsides to this. Management assumes that the people performing the work have nothing to add to it and any variance in behavior is punished swiftly. The system doesn't grow, change, evolve, or benefit from the observations of its staff. When it becomes outdated, it quickly disappears.

Most modern white collar and creative organizations employ a flatter management strategy. While there are tiers of management in these organizations, how you perform the tasks of your own job is much less regimented. The primary hallmarks of this are less supervision, greater accountability, and a tremendous need for mutual understanding[11]. A flat management strategy essentially tells each worker "you are here, you want to arrive there, please find the shortest path to your destination." Maybe you offer a roadmap as well, but each employee is trusted to create a system, held accountable to the results of their actions, and when outcomes don't meet expectations, it's usually the relationship that salvages mutual understanding and revised efforts. The primary downsides of this approach are that popular people tend to command undue influence, it is very difficult to resolve grievances adequately, and traditional, patriarchal, racist power structures

---

11 I once worked as a regulator for a major credit card company, where I had a job description but no actual work to do. I could do literally nothing, which had no impact on the organization. The company was required to have my job by the federal government.

recreate themselves quickly. In a flat organization that places high demands on any metric, employees will quickly feel forced into unethical behavior. For example, employees of Wells Fargo were forced to open a vast number of new accounts each month to keep their jobs and the material demands of this were impossible. They would sign up customers for new accounts and credit cards unknowingly, canceling them later, and trick elderly patrons into creating additional accounts. The federal government ended up fining them $185M for these practices and put tighter restrictions on their behavior.

For most organizations, you want to find a healthy balance that suits you between vertical and flat management. Ideally you want to give each person enough freedom to look at the problem, take your experience and data into account, and to create a mutually magnificent solution together. There is no one-size-fits-all solution for all businesses. While an ad agency would employ a flatter management strategy, food service really needs a fairly rigid hierarchy or recipes will be inconsistent. You want to create the right balance of systems, designated decision makers who are respected by your staff, and a clear understanding of why things operate the way that they do.

Your employees are your competitive advantage. They are the one thing that your competitors don't have and they form the fabric of your team. The emotional dynamics and space between them is often what motivates them to greatness. People are diligent and do a good job because they feel committed to how their actions affect their coworkers. For all of these reasons, in almost every case, retention is paramount. This isn't just because of the costs of training or that they would run away to share your trade secrets with your competitor or because their departure would despirit the rest of your staff. It's because in summation it makes more sense to keep someone as long they are working in tandem with your team. They already have your shared values, shared enthusiasm, willingness to work together, and can see your eventual goals and vision.

Retention is pretty easy if you listen. A recent study showed that working from home and flexible hours are so important to workers that the participants studied were willing to accept 10-40% lower pay if they could set their own hours from home! Yet many employers are resistant. For most workers quality of life is more important than money or benefits, so listening and being creative in your solutions will go a lot further than attempting to create a one-size-fits-all solution.

The only major exception to maintaining retention is if someone—even a high performer—is sowing discontent or endless negativity throughout your staff. It's okay for someone to have grievances, but if they don't address this with you—or worse, deny it to you but complain about it to everyone else so that you cannot resolve it—you need to set a firm boundary with the understanding that they will likely leave. We had an employee who began telling other members of our staff that while my income was lower than hers, that I made most of my money from speakers' fees that were a direct result of everyone's work. The reality is that all of the speakers' fees were kept within the organization to pay everyone's bonuses. When I asked her about this rumor, she dodged the question, citing that she just thought that we should "talk about it." When I pointed out that spreading false information without bringing concerns to me left no way to talk about it or resolve it, she dodged the issue again. A year later, her negativity had become directed towards the majority of our staff and she would frequently tell other people how to do their jobs, direct their resources, or simply how they were bad at their job. She was our highest performing employee but the costs of maintaining her constant path of wreckage were much greater than the benefits. When someone is behaving as both a bully and an energy vampire like this, draining everyone's patience away from doing their actual job, there is nothing that can justify it as worthwhile. The human resources manager and I had a phone call with her where we set a firm boundary about communicating with her coworkers. She compared us to Trump, hung up on us, and quit. It was difficult and sad that we couldn't resolve it, but it's better than letting a problem fester. Because when you do, you are communicating to the rest of your team that when someone violates a boundary, there are no consequences. Your team has to work as a unit, respect each other, and recognize that the goals are worth the short-term compromises. And sometimes, someone just isn't capable of doing the job that they were hired for and it's necessary to fire them. Sometimes it's harder to see the limitations of someone's skill set until they've made the same mistake a dozen times, just don't put enough attention to detail, aren't committed to doing things the way that you see fit, or believe that their ideas supersede yours. Sometimes it makes sense to move someone to a different department and if there's nowhere else to go, the best thing that you can do for both of you is to let them go. It's unfair to both of you to let someone fester doing their job badly over a longer period of time when they could excel elsewhere.

Another eerily common problem in business is dealing with the ghost of everyone's former employer. Everyone picks up emotional baggage from the way that they were treated in the past, and employees have this weird expectation that you will do the same shitty thing to them that their previous boss did. I have one direct report who came to work every time that she had a migraine for her first year because her previous boss said she would be fired if she missed work because of it. She did not do her best work with a migraine and we both would have been better off if she stayed home until she felt better. When we made postings about our growth and hiring for new job positions, some employees in those departments interpreted this announcement that they were being replaced. Their managers explained that growth is a good thing, that they will have help doing their jobs. In other cases, employees will be chronically convinced that you are trying to find new ways to screw them over or on the brink of going out of business—even if there are zero signs that it's happening and you are having a record year. Most employees expect their boss to micromanage every inch of their time—no matter how many times you explain how things work here. And hardest of all is convincing people that when you ask them a question, you want an honest answer—and that there are no "correct" answers besides their own truth. In one case, an employee told me that at her last job that when they needed to cut hours, they would poll the office about who wanted to go home early and anyone who raised their hand would receive a demerit on their record. They would only send people home early who did not want to go. These kinds of psychological warfare give all employers a bad name. Give your employees basic respect and honest communication. See that they are human beings with strengths and faults. Recognize that you have considerably more power. Allow yourselves to talk through problems together. With time they will overcome ways that they were treated wrongfully in the past and you will build trust together.

However, in some cases, you will have the very worst news. You are failing, or at least you are in a tailspin and need to cut your expenses. In these cases, the most important thing is to express appreciation for the person and their contributions over your time together. Yet, you cannot afford to keep them on payroll. Perhaps you are willing to be creative here. When I regained ownership of Microcosm and was burdened with the previous owner's debt load, two people were willing to stay even though none of us could get paid. So we established that in return for their continued labor, they would buy equity into ownership of the company. Ten years later, this proved to be a great choice. The value of their equity has grown 779%. Everybody won because we aligned the carrot and the stick.

SALES

Selling is scary at first, but if you prepare and do your homework, the work will do itself. Remember, you are solving a problem, so the litmus test is reaching the people who need that problem solved and your ability to explain it to them. Let's break it down to its simplest parts.

Listen to people. I once received a phone call from a carpet cleaner. I promptly informed him that my entire house was hardwood and tile and there were no carpets to clean. I had no problems that he could solve. I expected him to understand that even if I wanted his service, there was no way to turn me into a customer. Instead, he began talking over me. Assuming that he misunderstood, I repeated myself. His volume continued to escalate. I began laughing and then hung up. He was employing the wrong strategy and wasting both of our time. Similarly, I frequently find myself behind our booth at an event where someone walks up and says "Are these kids' books?" and ignores me when I respond "no" and then begins to tell me that they wish they had brought their kids because their kids might like some of these books, despite just explaining that these were very much not appropriate for children. Ask questions to draw out people's confusion or assumptions. Helping them to see what problem that you are solving will help them to see if they are a good fit. If a potential customer says "email me on Monday and we'll schedule a meeting," it means "we aren't having this conversation right now, but I am interested." Respect that. They might be blowing you off but you should follow up anyway because it shows that you are listening and can follow directions. You may not get the sale this time but showing that you aren't a pain to work with will get you the sale in the future if the customer is right for you. Respect people, mind the instructions, and follow through. That's how you win. Find the nuance and respect their wishes.

You can't steamroll someone's rejection or lack of interest. I receive a dozen emails every day proclaiming "I am following up on my previous offers," without any context about what they *are offering*. Remind me about your value proposition and create a pleasant environment. I'd say "This is Joe from Microcosm. We talked about bringing in some books to your store a few months ago and you asked for samples. Which ones did you like?" Leave pauses for them to offer feedback. They want to be the ones to resume conversation. I've watched more people fail by giving the hard sell than succeed. Give your customers enough respect to determine if they are interested in what you are doing. They will thank you for it. With space, they can figure out if it's of interest—if not to themselves, then to their customers or a close friend. If they say no, thank them for their time and interest. Send a handwritten thank you note as a follow up. Because this is so rare, people will take notice and remember you. They might not purchase right now, but they will keep a note of you and tuck you away for later.

Most people communicate interest in ways other than making an immediate purchase or declaring their undying love for your work. Though, at one event, we did have two separate, adult customers who broke out crying because they were so overjoyed that we were there. So don't rule anything out. However, most people express interest through nonverbal cues, such as remaining on the phone with you and asking questions or prolonging a moment. Sometimes they want to know what it would be like to work with you. They may want to feel involved because they emotionally relate to your values, ideas, worldview, and personal expression. This is one reason why it's important not to spend that time complaining or badmouthing a coworker in front of a customer. You don't want to repel people by giving them a negative or inaccurate representation of who you are.

Learn from each and every rejection, even if the lesson is that certain people aren't your customer. Don't spend your time focusing on people who will never be happy with your passionate creations. Spend your time focusing on people who *love* what you do. Sometimes the lesson is where you should or should not be. Focus on people whom you might have failed or who have developmental ideas that would make things work better. Listen to feedback and take it to heart. If you're making beverages, for example, the most important things are your flavors, your ingredients, and your packaging. Often, the right person's lack of interest signifies that you aren't explaining yourself quite right on the bottle. A mentor once imparted the wisdom that the job is figuring out which half of feedback you get to listen to. But even rejections, like emotions, contain information. It is, however, your job to distill the usable portion out and incorporate it into your future approach.

Create a sales funnel, a way to introduce new people to what you are doing.

- For years, we partnered with local nonprofits to organize touring events. We'd bring stock from our bookstore to sell on those tours as well as a cookbook author to make dinner. We'd give out a coupon to the audience to use on our website. This produced a lot of repeat customers who previously were not familiar with us. We distributed endless promotional materials along the way. Over 20 years, we introduced hundreds of thousands of prospective readers to the wide end of the funnel every year. The successful dissemination of this information is called the "**Awareness**" stage.

- Some people are immediately captivated by at least our mission and some of our titles. This is called the "**Interest**" stage. They may not be readers, though they might buy our books as presents for others.

- If they linger at our table or on our website long enough, they are hovering at the "**Consideration**" stage. They may need some questions answered or need a discount or it may take them a bit longer to understand the payoff of our books and how they might benefit their own lives.

- Finally, a select few make the decision that our books are worth the money at the "**Action**" stage. The people who reach these final two stages are those that you want to focus your effort around because they are the most likely to keep coming back for more. Give them reasons to. Tell them about new ideas and initiatives. Help them feel involved. Many of the people who discovered our books over twenty years ago at these events are still our customers today.

Your funnel might be events, or it could also be social media, an email newsletter, flyers you leave in public places, a word of mouth campaign, or all of the above.

Confidence is the result of knowledge and practice but you have to fake it before you make it.

I've certainly seen people have confidence with no knowledge or practice. I have seen people who only have one or the other. We once had a new salesperson at work sit down and begin making calls and then with each call, she would put the customer on hold and ask "Okay, how do I input the order? What is the discount? Do they have to pay up front?" It was incredible to watch her work and be unflappable through eight hours of cold calls and rejections. She was very confident because she was experienced, even if she didn't have the knowledge yet. You can harness what you do possess to make up for the parts that you haven't mastered yet.

You need to embody a bit of each of these ideas and skills. Some of them will be difficult to understand until you have more practice and experience. The important thing is to be enthusiastic and leave people with a positive encounter from interacting with you, giving them enough space to ask questions.

SERVICE

One of the greatest paradoxes in customer service is the way that you earn trust by repairing a mistake. Customers respond *more* favorably to you when you make a mistake and fix it with grace than when you never make a mistake. And you will make mistakes. If you haven't yet, it's only because you haven't had enough opportunities to or haven't been busy enough yet. But before long, you will screw up. And this will be your first test.

When I bought a pair of cycling shoes that had soles so slick that I fell off my bike pedals in the rain, the customer service employee was clearly reading a script to me. His solution didn't make great sense. They wanted to give me a 40% off coupon to buy an additional pair of shoes with the understanding that I gave up my right to file a suit and now understood that not all of their shoes are great for cycling, but might be better for walking. I recognized that this solution meant that I could buy several other high priced items at a massive savings. So while it doesn't make sense from the point of my stated problem, it gave me a more favorable view of the company that they took it seriously.

You will ship the wrong item or to the wrong address or bill someone incorrectly or the item will mysteriously never arrive. In cases like these, you never want to get defensive. It's irrelevant if it's your fault or not. You simply want to solve the problem. This means that you restate what the customer tells you went wrong in order to empathize and show that you understand, you apologize, then you propose a solution that addresses it. If you can do this each and every time that you make a mistake, people will feel closer to you because you can solve their problems.

Let's take a look at some very basic best practices:

- Have a human being answer your phones and respond to your messages

- Only make promises that you can (and will) keep

- Establish a system for hearing and addressing problems

- When numerous customers have the same problem, address the issue at its root.

- You want to make 80% of customers happy, even if you lose money on a few sales. You want them to come back next time.

- The other 20% of customers will never be happy and you don't want to cultivate them to keep coming back for more problems you will lose money on.

- Establish systems and service solution parameters for your staff to implement so that there is never a question about how to handle a standard situation.

When a company screws up and repairs the situation—exceeding expectations—customers are much more likely to respond favorably, talk about the company to their friends and family, and continue to do business. There are numerous famous examples of this. In one case a house painting company got some paint on a family's carpet. In response, they paid for new carpet in the family's entire home. Why? Because they knew that the family and the press would be talking about this incident for years to come and it would make them the first choice for other families to hire. Keep your budgets reasonable but consider leverage in all of your service decisions.

How much of a relationship do you have? How much of a relationship do you want?

When you see a problem, start working on a solution right away—even before someone tells you that there is a problem. That might be a problem that is preventing someone from buying something or getting it home or deciding between a few items or colors. Problem solving can help you think quickly on your feet, keep the situation positive, and foster other vital skills in a fast-moving environment where you are on public display.

MONEY AND INVESTMENT

A loan company once called me with the pitch, "Who wants to spend their own money?" Of course, they neglected to mention the annual cost of interest. The type of business that you are operating will determine if it's preferable to reinvest your own money to fund your own growth or to borrow money to do this. Other factors to consider are how interest is tax deductible and the best uses for your own cash, versus the directions that you need to grow into for your own, specific goals.

Similarly, factors outside of your control determine if you should own or rent. In some regions, ownership is simply impossible. Whereas in others, ownership is much cheaper, creating cost savings for years to come and insulating you from the costs of inflation.

Think of money as a stepping stone to the places that you want to go to. When you're spending each dollar, it should benefit you in three ways:

- Providing you a good or service that you need (like raw materials or staffing)

- Directing you towards specific, identified goals

- Incentives like credit card cash back rewards or travel benefits, like free hotels or flights

This should inform both everyday decisions and big picture strategy. If your goals are reasonable and broken down properly into steps, spending towards them will move the needle towards them. Create metrics for how to measure the effectiveness of each dollar spent. Does it increase sales? Does it decrease future expenses? Will it help you to turn the corner to expand your market share?

A healthy budget should be revisited monthly, evaluated honestly, and have adequate tools for analyzing every dollar that you spend and its effectiveness. For example, if a third of your budget is inventory and you're spending more than you're earning every month, it's time to cut back on inventory. When the price of boxes skyrocketed in 2021, it was a great time to reuse boxes that we received in our warehouses. And mostly importantly, what budget reallocations would it take in order to be able to finance your own growth? Doing so is usually far preferable, because you eliminate risks and can already see the need for it as well as the potential.

Loans are useful, but only insofar as they take you where you want to go and are mutually beneficial.

Similarly, when operations run behind schedule, you need to determine if this is a temporary setback or a new normal and you need to expand staffing. Sometimes, even if you *are* running behind, this is preferable to increasing expenses in that department. Create metrics to know when you should add capacity or square footage to your operation. Sometimes it's simply your location that's not working and you need to move. What seems more expensive on paper can unlock a lot of new opportunities.

As a small business, minding the amount of money that you receive each day versus what you pay out each day is essential. You can't function on theoretical or borrowed money forever. In general, you should only take risks when you have to or you can see that the opportunity from doing so could be tremendous. For example, I realized that while it would stretch us thin to purchase our office building in 2012, the opportunity gave us a fixed real estate cost after watching these costs slowly climb over decades—and costs skyrocketed shortly thereafter. Buying would not have been possible even a few years later.

RULES, LAWS, AND TAXES

No matter your industry, there are governing apparatuses that are bigger than you and out of your control. If you have a restaurant, food temperatures are regulated by random visits from the health inspector. If you have a club, the fire inspector will be by before long to make sure that exits are visibly marked and accessible. If you are a therapist or doctor, state review boards oversee how ethically you do your job.

There is also the inevitability of taxes. You will pay city, county, state, transit, federal, sales, employment, and innumerable other types of taxes. Familiarize yourself before you get started and utilize tools like Gusto that make these filings and payments on your behalf.

There are far too many intricacies and specifics to go into here and they vary widely by industry. So the best that you can do is talk to other people in your profession to get a sense of what surprises awaited them and how to prepare yourself now.

DEALING WITH MONOPOLIES

*I*nternet telecom companies are notorious for their terrible service. This is because they have a veritable monopoly on providing it. The last time I signed an internet agreement, my provider immediately began charging me triple the agreed upon price. I had to cancel service in order to get them to follow our contract. Their costs of installation and the need to register as many users as possible in my neighborhood to justify the infrastructure costs are the only reasons they were forced to work with me. I would never willingly give money every month to CenturyLink for fiber optic internet—except I have no choice because they are the only company that installed lines in my neighborhood. I call this "the monopoly problem."

The monopoly problem can infect smaller companies too. There are very few companies in the U.S. that produce screen-printed vinyl stickers, which allows each of them to get away with various strange quirks. One takes months to print any order. Another cannot respond to an email or a phone call or keep a promise. A third has terrible quality and worse excuses when you ask them to reprint. But all three pale in comparison to the company who confirmed my order but did not tell me that I needed to pay in advance to get my job printed. Two months later, when I checked in on when it would ship, the owner asked to talk on the phone. He spent ten minutes yelling about how great he is at communicating. Irony aside, behavior like this is only prompted by the idea you have plenty of customers and they have few alternatives. Midway into his extended rant, I asked, "Do you think this conversation is going to make our relationship better or worse?" This question sent him down another spiral. My position that he needed to tell me to pay in order to get my job into production seemed to cast serious doubts on his self-image. Seemingly, he could only resolve this through telling me how wrong I was at top volume.

For some reason or another, we don't do business together anymore, but I did develop a new question when evaluating a potential new working relationship: "Would this person call to yell at me for ten minutes about how I am wrong?" And, you know, it's amazing how that question puts things into perspective. You *can* make that determination about someone pretty quickly. For a monopoly, a relationship is a one-way street. They tightened the value chain and the control points too far. They dictate the terms of the agreement to you and if you question this, they may explode at you. There's not a lot that you can do in these cases other than building a substantive relationship with the company of your choice and maintaining it aggressively. Establish mutual goodwill so that they are motivated to resolve problems quickly, or at all.

VENDORS AND SUPPLIERS

Fortunately, you don't run into monopolies too often. Much more common is finding yourself working with a supplier that is simply unmanaged. They're held together seemingly by duct tape, bailing wire, and one competent employee who quit last week, and you'll often find yourself having to correct their mistakes.

We import numerous books from Europe to distribute in the U.S. These come from British warehouses, are handled across the pond by a freight forwarder, and are deposited into a warehouse in Pennsylvania where we arrange transportation to our warehouse in Cleveland. Except, in every single case as of this writing, we arranged our own shipper to pick up and deliver them to us, yet the pallets of books were nowhere to be found! The freight forwarder had accidentally shipped them already with their own carrier—in two cases, 2,700 miles past their destination to our office in Oregon and back! Now there are lots of freight companies and my first step was to talk to our European partners to ask them to switch freight forwarders. Turns out they have this problem all the time and had already been considering changing companies. But what if they hadn't?

You want to treat an unmanaged company that you have a business relationship with like a child who is acting out. The only difference is that, in the case of the business, no one is in charge. My basic script is "What caused this? How will it be fixed moving forward? What will happen if it continues?" A conversation like this solves 90% of ongoing problems. They may think you are being unreasonable, but they see that you are serious, that there is a problem, and that you could stop working together.

Some cases, however, are more extreme. We worked with a company who routinely made payment mistakes of $10,000 per month in their own favor. They would record a credit as a debit on their ledger and when we would point out their mistake, they would condescendingly say "Well, these statements can be really complicated. If it would help, we can have someone explain it to you." Obviously, the problem isn't the complication, but that we had to diligently check their work every time. And every statement revealed additional errors, always in their favor. They believed that they controlled a monopoly on their industry, yet they had more competitors than they realized. We eventually had our lawyer take care of it and they paid us three separate settlement payments on top of interest and what they owed us because apparently it really is complicated for them to get it right!

Fortunately, most problems don't escalate in this manner. We have another company who bills us incorrectly about 25% of the time. So we added a clause to our agreement that if they supply incorrect billing, we charge $25 per page. This was partially meant as a joke to motivate them to check their work and send us accurate bills, but their systems are really clunky and cumbersome. So instead, they pay us several thousand dollars per year because they would rather outsource their billing department to us. Creative solutions can solve a problem like this even if people can't get their act together and it doesn't turn out quite like you expected it to.

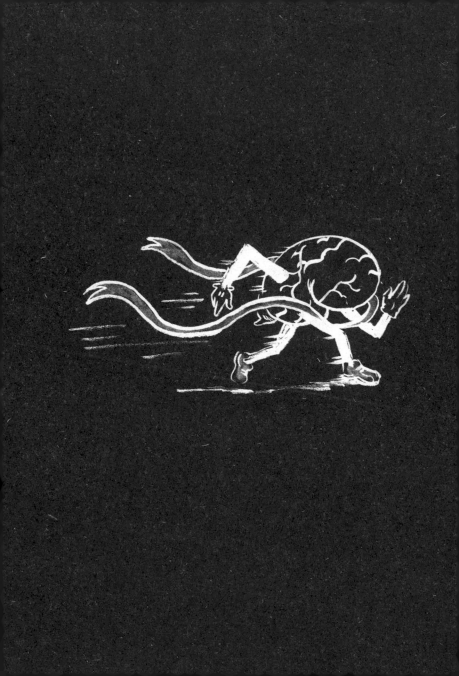

THE LAST MILE

One of the most common things that plague businesses is the "Last Mile Problem." Think of lost sales from customers waiting in a long line at a restaurant[12] or the costs of a food delivery.[13] In short, more than half of the costs of a good are often in the final steps of reaching the customer. Just like more than half of the cost of fiber optic cable is drilling it from the street into your basement, the most difficult aspects of anything are in the last mile. After pallets travel thousands of miles in a matter of days, they have at times sat for weeks in the local delivery center, a mere mile from our warehouse, waiting for a driver to be headed in our direction. Once we had a delivery driver insist on parking a block away from our delivery gate because he was inexperienced and didn't want to have to turn around after turning onto our side street. Not only was he parked blocking the

---

12 A restaurant in my neighborhood turned this into marketing by moving that line outside and providing refreshments and umbrellas, to show passersby how popular the restaurant is! The appearance of popularity makes you think it *must* be good!

13 Why services like Grubhub, Postmates, UberEats, or Delivered Dish are heavily in demand and expensive—yet they still cannot make a profit. Similarly, most restaurant's lowest net sales are deliveries because they have to absorb this expense. Food delivery is virtually required because it's expected by customers but there are few ways to actually charge consumers what it costs, due to competition.

bus, but the extra distance meant that our staff spent an additional 90 minutes moving the books inside. His carrier tried to bill us extra for his time. You can sell things in another country with cryptocurrency, but then the hardest part can be finding a way to convert it to your local currency. One reason for this is that no matter what you do, for the first 90% of your product's journey, you benefit from bundling. When we order books from our printer, they are all shipped to our warehouse with lots of other packages going to other warehouses. As we take them apart and ship out thousands of smaller packages, some of those get lost in the mail or returned. It's simply more efficient to have thousands of packages in a delivery vehicle and the minute that you are making special trips to each person's house with their ecommerce purchases, it's remarkably less efficient than delivering hundreds of boxes to a retailer where customers walk in and buy what they crave. Last mile problems are unique and specific to your exact business. The important thing is to be mindful of them, consider different approaches that you can take, and understand that the last mile is half of your cost. Think of a clever solution like the restaurant line.

CONCLUSION

The most important thing as you grow is to resist becoming set in your ways. Things change, situations evolve, and cultural dynamics have major breakthroughs. Be willing to try new things and even old things that didn't work before. That is, as long as they serve your broadest strategic goals.

The most important thing, as in any part of life, is to be open to continuing to learn every day. Things that worked out great in the past will not be that way forever. Events that were terrible in the past may involve factors that will change and become a great fit. I had a table at a literary conference in 2006 where people turned up their noses at me and wouldn't give me the time of day. By the time it came back to my city thirteen years later, the organizers had modernized the event and made it much more compatible with our brand of publishing. I built a much larger presence and it became our highest netting event of the year. Now we plan every year around it!

It's important to believe that you deserve what you want. Otherwise it becomes far too easy to deprive yourself of the results that you've pushed so hard for and the outcome that you deserve. It's easy to situate yourself as a big fish in a small pond, working weekends on top of your regular job to pursue a craft that you love, but is there room to grow your passion bigger? Intellectual or emotional limitations are usually self-imposed and can put the lowest ceiling on your operation.

Take what you are doing very seriously so that others can see how cool it is. Remember that you chose something that you believe in. Let others see your enthusiasm. I've often met people who didn't care much about books but bought our books because they could see how much they meant to me and wanted a little piece of that for their home.

Remember, people resonate with how they felt interacting with you far more than what they bought. You wouldn't believe how many times I'll be at an event where someone shouts "I love Microcosm!" and when I ask basic reporter questions, like "Cool! Which book is your favorite?" you'd be surprised how often they respond, "Oh, I don't think I actually own any of your books. Huh." Still, that person has warm feelings for us, which means that we've done our job and certainly when they see something of ours that they do resonate with, we've already bridged the gap. And you can too!

Everything is difficult in the moment. It isn't difficult *after* the moment. Keep this in mind as you are making difficult decisions. They won't always be difficult and they will seem obvious later, to be replaced by new and exciting challenges!

RECOMMENDED READING

Blue Ocean Strategy: How to Create Uncontested Market Space and Make Competition Irrelevant by W. Chan Kim and Renée Mauborgne

The Carrot and the Stick: Leveraging Strategic Control for Growth by William Putsis

The Gift of Fear: And Other Survival Signals that Protect Us from Violence by Gavin De Becker

Growing a Business by Paul Hawken

Dare to Lead: Brave Work. Tough Conversations. Whole Hearts. by Brené Brown

Decoded by Jay-Z

High-Output Management by Andy Grove

The Listening Path: The Creative Art of Attention by Julie Cameron

Never Split The Difference: Negotiating as if Your Life Depended on It by Christopher Voss and Tahl Raz

People Skills: How to Assert Yourself, Listen to Others, and Resolve Conflicts by Robert Bolton

A People's Guide to Publishing: Build a Successful, Sustainable, Meaningful Book Business by Joe Biel

Unfuck Your Worth: Overcome Your Money Emotions, Value Your Own Labor, and Manage Financial Freakouts in a Capitalist Hellscape by Dr. Faith G. Harper

Unfuck Your Boundaries: Build Better Relationships through Consent, Communication, and Expressing Your Needs by Dr. Faith G. Harper

What Every Body Is Saying: An Ex-FBI Agent's Guide to Speed Reading People by Joe Navarro

CITATIONS

Cameron, J. (2021). The listening path: The creative art of attention. St. Martin's Essentials.

Diamandis, P. H., & Kotler, S. (2017). Bold: How to go big, create wealth and impact the world. Simon & Schuster.

Grove, A. S. (2015). High output management. Vintage Books.

Hawken, P. (2006). Growing a business. Simon and Schuster Paperbacks.

Kim, W. C., & Mauborgne, R. (2016). Blue Ocean Strategy: How to create uncontested market space and make the competition irrelevant. Harvard Bus Review Press.

Putsis, W. (2020). The Carrot and the stick: Leveraging strategic control for growth. University of Toronto Press.

Research: Perspective-taking doesn't help you understand what others want. Harvard Business Review. (2018, October 9). Retrieved October 25, 2022, from https://hbr.org/2018/10/research-perspective-taking-doesnt-help-you-understand-what-others-want